performance practice:

a bibliography

performance practice:
a bibliography

Edited by Mary Vinquist

and Neal Zaslaw

W · W · NORTON & COMPANY · INC · *NEW YORK*

Prepared for book publication by L. Michael Griffel

SBN   393   02148   3   (Cloth Edition)
SBN   393   00550   X   (Paper Edition)

Library of Congress Catalog Card No. 75–128038

Published simultaneously in Canada
by George J. McLeod Limited, Toronto

Printed in the United States of America

1 2 3 4 5 6 7 8 9 0

contents

Ever since the pioneer publication of J. N. Forkel's *Allgemeine Literatur der Musik* (1792) music scholars have been striving to achieve bibliographical control over the literature of music. We have recently witnessed great strides in this aspect of our field, with such important undertakings as the *Répertoire International des Sources Musicales*, the *Répertoire International de Littérature Musicale*, and *Die Musik in Geschichte und Gegenwart*.[1] Yet in spite of these advances, scholars know only too well that many a worthwhile and needed research project has been postponed or abandoned because of the difficulty of locating the materials to be studied. It is now widely accepted, for instance, that the writing of the history of music of the second half of the 18th century in a manner other than superficial must await proper bibliographical organization of the vast musical, literary, and archival sources involved.[2] And while the writing of interpretative historical essays must continue to be the domain of single scholars, the compilation of comprehensive catalogues and bibliographies can well be carried out—following the example of the physical and social sciences—by group effort.

This book will, I hope, serve as a case in point. Its genesis was as follows: Professor William S. Newman of the University of North Carolina had found that his *Seminar on Performance Practices* required an extensive bibliography on that subject and that none existed. As his graduate students set to work on this project, he wrote to me (in my capacity as Editor of *Current Musicology*) asking if we were interested in publishing such a bibliography. My initial inquiries among musical *Kenner und Liebhaber* revealed such a strongly-felt need for the project that I immediately wrote back to Professor Newman urging that his students prepare the bibliography for publication. When the manuscript (edited by one of the North Carolina graduate students, Mary Vinquist) was received, I checked, revised, and edited it with the considerable assistance of the fellow graduate students at Columbia University who formed the staff of *Current Musicology*. The resulting version was proofread at both North Carolina and Columbia and published in 1969.[3] Meanwhile a second group of Professor Newman's graduate students had prepared a considerable supplement to the first bibliography, which was edited at North Carolina by Marcia Citron, revised at Columbia again, proofread at both schools, and published in 1970.[4] The present book represents the cumulation of both bibliographies in a uniform, integrated format, and owes much to the labors of L. Michael Griffel, my successor as Editor of *Current Musicology*.

The many contributors to this cooperative venture need be acknowledged. The members of the first seminar at North Carolina were June Burbage, G. Kenneth Cooper, Don C. Gillespie, Lynda G. Houghland, G. Philip Koonce, William K. Miller, Charles F. T. Nakarai, Rudi Schnitzler, William B. Stacy, and Mary Vinquist. The members of the second seminar were Kathy Boardman, Nancy Boyd, Donna Certain, Marcia Citron, Don

Coleman, Ted Gossett, Susan Harden, Jeff Ishee, Tom Jenrette, Heasun Kim, Susan Kincaid, Donna Laney, Pamela Levy, Christine Ligo, Gary Maas, Susan Patrick, and Don Skelton. The Columbia editors for the first bibliography were Alex Blachly, Kathryn Bumpass, Shai Burstyn, Josephine Mongiardo Cooper, L. Michael Griffel, Margaret Ross Griffel, Joan Long, and Mary Obelkevich. For the supplement the associate editor was Josephine Mongiardo Cooper.

The compilers of this bibliography do not agree wholly with Willi Apel's characterization of their subject. Performance practice, writes Apel, is "the study of how early music from the Middle Ages to Bach was performed and the many problems connected with attempts to restore its original sound in modern performance."[5] The suggested termination of the study of performance practices with Bach is an arbitrary and fallacious limitation. This fallacy arises from the notion that because we have grown up in a musical tradition in which the music of the Classical and Romantic periods is constantly studied, taught, and performed, we must already know the "original sound" intended by the composers of that music. To take just one familiar example, the performance of Mozart's music is the subject of a sizeable literature (seventy-six entries in the index of this book), and styles of Mozart performance have changed considerably during the last quarter century under the impact of those studies.

The limits for inclusion or exclusion of items in this bibliography were dictated by considerations of what would be useful to the largest number of its readers and by the practical need to keep the project down to a reasonable size. The scope and format sought by the North Carolina seminar were summarized by Mary Vinquist as follows:[6]

> . . . we restricted ourselves to Western art music between roughly 1100 and 1900. Furthermore, with a few exceptions, we did not include plainsong, notation (including tablature), *musica ficta*, solmisation, *musica reservata*, sociology and psychology, liturgics, discography, editions confined only to music, references to misprints, present-day pedagogy, aesthetics, instrument construction, iconography, and reviews. . . . Questions of structure and style [proved] so elusive that they were of necessity eliminated at the outset. Our intentions were to investigate problems of the "how-to-do-it" kind. . . . If these excluded categories seem almost to eliminate the bibliography, we should hasten to add that we do include problems immediately concerned with the actual performance of music. . . .

> Materials were drawn from the English, German, French, Italian, Spanish, and Dutch languages only. Since most entries include musical examples, only examples of unusual interest are cited here. Annotations are provided except where topics are adequately indicated in the titles. Annotations are also necessarily omitted in titles of items that could not be seen before this bibliography went to press. Where possible, names are spelled as in *Baker's Biographical Dictionary*, 5th Edition and Supplement. If no author is known, an entry begins with the title. For alpha-

4

betization purposes, umlauts are treated as if the missing "e" were present.

This bibliography includes the contents of all earlier bibliographies on the subject and adds to that a considerable amount of new material. It is above all a working tool for music scholars, students, performers, and listeners. Like any practical tool, it serves some purposes well and others not at all. It can be counted on to indicate a substantial portion of the studies on a given topic, and the examination of those studies can be expected in turn to lead farther afield to additional sources. The bibliography cannot, however, be expected to generate an exhaustive list of works on any topic, since that is precluded by the essentially inexhaustible nature of the sources and the fact that important points in performance practice will always have to be gleaned from sources not fundamentally concerned with that subject. The user of this bibliography is further cautioned that no attempt has been made to list all of the editions and reprints of those publications which have enjoyed such successes; the bibliography, therefore, is a tool for learning of the existence of publications relating to performance practice, but not for assembling comprehensive histories of their republication.

Every effort has been made to offer a reasonably representative and accurate bibliography, and only the test of use will reveal fully its perfections and imperfections. But whether or not Matthew Arnold was right that "the pursuit of perfection is the pursuit of sweetness and light," it is the hope of the compilers and editors of this book that, whatever its imperfections may be, it will sweeten and lighten the labors of all those who study or perform the music of the past.

NEAL ZASLAW
Ithaca, N.Y.
December, 1970

NOTES

1 For an accounting of recent important bibliographical accomplishments in musicology, see the introduction to the second edition of *Music Reference and Research Materials* by Vincent Duckles (New York, 1967).

2 For some of the difficulties facing the would-be historian of 18th-century music, see the articles by Gerald Abraham, Vincent Duckles, Donald Jay Grout, Daniel Heartz, Jan LaRue, Leonard G. Ratner, and J. A. Westrup *in* "18th-Century Studies in Honor of Paul Henry Lang," *Current Musicology*, Issue Number 9/1969.

3 It occupies the entirety of *Current Musicology*, Issue Number 8/1969.

4 In *Current Musicology* (1970) 10:144–72.

5 "Performance Practice," *The Harvard Dictionary of Music*, 2nd edition (Cambridge, 1969).

6 Excerpts quoted from *Current Musicology* (1969) 8:9 and (1970) 10:62.

a bibliography of performance practice bibliographies

Some previous bibliographies of writings on performance practices are listed below rather than in the main list. But not listed below are the bibliographies in such overall works as those by Donington, Haas, and Dart, as well as numerous other entries in which general performance practice bibliographies are cited in the annotations.

"Bibliography of Handel Performance Practice," Händel Jb (1933) 131–34, (1955) 132–33.

Coover, James. "Music Theory in Translation: A Bibliography," *Journal of Music Theory* III (1959) 70–96. (incl. many *b. c.* treatises).

Ferand, Ernest T. "Didactic Embellishment Literature in the Late Renaissance: A Survey of Sources," Festschrift REESE 154–72.

Garretson, Homer Eugene. "An Annotated Bibliography of Written Material Pertinent to the Performance of Chamber Music for Stringed Instruments," unpublished Ed.D. diss., University of Illinois, 1961. (Eng., Fr., and Ger. language periodicals; books since 1900).

Rutan, Harold Duane. "An Annotated Bibliography of Written Material Pertinent to the Performance of Brass and Percussion Chamber Music," unpublished Ed.D. diss., University of Illinois, 1960.

Sasse, Konrad (ed.). *Händel Bibliographie.* Leipzig: VEB Deutscher Verlag für Musik, 1963, 254–64.

Schmidt, Lloyd John. "A Practical and Historical Source-Book for the Recorder," unpublished Ph.D. diss., Northwestern University, 1959.

Schmieder, Wolfgang, in BJ XL (1933) 145–47, XLV (1958) 140–42.

Squire, Alan Paul. "An Annotated Bibliography of Written Material Pertinent to the Performance of Woodwind Chamber Music," unpublished Ed.D. diss., University of Illinois, 1960 (Fr. and Ger. listings not annotated).

Warner, Thomas E. *An Annotated Bibliography of Woodwind Instruction Books, 1600–1830.* Detroit: Information Coordinators, Inc., 1967 (incl. locales of each tutor).

AfMf	Archiv für Musikforschung
AfMw	Archiv für Musikwissenschaft
AMl	Acta Musicologica
AMS Papers	Papers of the American Musicological Society
AmZ	Allgemeine musikalische Zeitung
AMz	Allgemeine Musikzeitung
AnM	Anuario Musical
AnnMl	Annales Musicologiques
AR	The American Recorder
Bachgedenkschrift	*Bach-Gedenkschrift, 1950: im Auftrag der Internationalen Bach-Gesellschaft,* ed. by K. Matthaei. Zurich: Atlantis, 1950
BAMS	Bulletin of the American Musicological Society
b. c.	basso continuo
Beethoven Jb	Beethoven-Jahrbuch
BJ	Bach-Jahrbuch
BQ	Brass Quarterly
BzMw	Beiträge zur Musikwissenschaft
DDT	Denkmäler deutscher Tonkunst
DTB	Denkmäler der Tonkunst in Bayern
DTÖ	Denkmäler der Tonkunst in Österreich
ed.	editor, edited, edition, edited by
EdM	Das Erbe deutscher Musik
esp.	especially
ex(x).	example(s)
ExpertMMFR	Expert, H., *Monuments de la Musique française au temps de la Renaissance*
ExpertMMRF	Expert, H., *Les Maîtres Musiciens de la Renaissance française*
fac.	facsimile
Festschrift ADLER	*Studien zur Musikgeschichte. Festschrift für Guido Adler zum 75. Geburtstag.* Vienna: Universal, 1930
Festschrift ANGLÉS	*Miscellánea en homenaje a Monseñor Higinio Anglés.* Barcelona: Consejo Superior de Investigaciones Científicas, 1958–61
Festschrift BACH-PROBLEME	*Bach-Probleme, Festschrift zur deutschen Bach-Feier, Leipzig, 1950,* ed. by H. Draeger and K. Laux. Leipzig: C. F. Peters, 1950
Festschrift DAVISON	*Essays on Music in Honor of Archibald Thompson Davison by His Associates.* Cambridge: Harvard University, Dept. of Music, 1957

Festschrift FELLERER	*Festschrift Karl Gustav Fellerer zum sechzigsten Geburtstag am 7. July 1962 überreicht von Freunden und Schülern,* ed. by H. Hüschen. Regensburg: Gustav Bosse, 1962
Festschrift HAYDON	*Studies in Musicology: Essays in the History, Style, and Bibliography of Music in Memory of Glen Haydon,* ed. by J. W. Pruett. Chapel Hill: University of North Carolina Press, 1969
Festschrift MARINUZZI	*L'Orchestra* [*in onore Gino Marinuzzi 1882–1945*]. Florence: G. Barbera, 1954
Festschrift PAUMGARTNER	*Wissenschaft und Praxis, eine Festschrift zum 70. Geburtstag von Bernhard Paumgartner.* [Zürich]: Atlantis Verlag, [1957?]
Festschrift RAABE	*Von deutscher Tonkunst. Festschrift zu Peter Rabbes 70. Geburtstag; in Gemeinschaft mit dreiundzwanzig Fachgenossen,* ed. by A. Morgenroth. Leipzig: Peters, [1942]
Festschrift REESE	*Aspects of Medieval and Renaissance Music: A Birthday Offering to Gustave Reese,* ed. by J. LaRue, *et al.* New York: W. W. Norton, 1966
Festschrift RIEMANN	*Riemann-Festschrift. Gesammelte Studien; Hugo Riemann zum sechzigsten Geburtstage überreicht von Freunden und Schülern.* Leipzig: M. Hesse, 1909
Festschrift SANDBERGER	*Festschrift zum 50. Geburtstag Adolf Sandburger überreicht von seinen Schülern.* Munich: Ferdinand Zierfuss, 1918
Festschrift SCHMIDT-GÖRG (60)	*Festschrift Joseph Schmidt-Görg zum 60. Geburtstag; Gemeinsam mit seinen Kollegen, Schülern und Freunden im Auftrag des Beethovenhauses,* ed. by D. Weise. Bonn: Beethovenhaus, 1957
Festschrift SCHMIDT-GÖRG (70)	*Colloquium amicorum: Joseph Schmidt-Görg zum 70. Geburtstag,* ed. by S. Kross and H. Schmidt. Bonn: Beethovenhaus, 1967
Festschrift SCHNEIDER (80)	*Festschrift Max Schneider zum achtzigsten Geburts- tage; in Verbindung mit Franz von Glasenapp, Ursula Schneider und Walther Siegmund-Schultze,* ed. by W. Vetter. Leipzig: Deutscher Verlag für Musik, [1955]
Festschrift STEIN	*Festschrift Fritz Stein zum 60. Geburtstag überreicht von Fachgenossen, Freunden und Schülern,* ed. by H. Hoffman and Fr. Rühlmann. Braunschweig: H. Litolff, 1939
Festschrift WOLF	*Musikwissenschaftliche Beiträge. Festschrift für Johannes Wolf zu seinem sechzigsten Geburtstag,*

8

	ed. by W. Lott, H. Osthoff and W. Wolffheim. Berlin: M. Breslauer, 1929
Gluck Jb	Gluck-Jahrbuch
Grove D	Grove, Dictionary of Music and Musicians
GSJ	Galpin Society Journal
Händel Jb	Händel-Jahrbuch
Händel Festspiele	*Festschrift der Händelfestspiele Halle.* Leipzig: Deutscher Verlag für Musik, 1954–56
incl.	includes
JAMS	Journal of the American Musicological Society
JbP	Jahrbücher der Musikbibliothek Peters
JRME	Journal of Research in Music Education
KmJb	Kirchenmusikalisches Jahrbuch
KONGRESS 1911 (London)	*Report of the Fourth Congress of the International Musical Society, London, 29th May–3rd June, 1911.* London: Novello & Co., 1912
KONGRESS 1925 (Leipzig)	*Bericht über den I. Musikwissenschaftlichen Kongress der Deutschen Musikgesellschaft in Leipzig vom 4. bis 8. Juni 1925.* Leipzig: Breitkopf & Härtel, 1926
KONGRESS 1930 (Liège)	*Report . . . International Society for Musical Research First Congress Liège September 1–6, 1930.* Burnham, Bucks: Plainsong & Mediaeval Music Society, [1930]
KONGRESS 1938 (Florence)	*Atti del terzo Congresso internazionale di Musica, Firenze, 30 Aprile–4 Maggio 1938–XVI.* Florence: Felice le Monnier, 1938
KONGRESS 1949 (Basel)	*Report . . . International Musicological Society Fourth Congress Basel June 29–July 3, 1949.* Basel: Bärenreiter-Verlag, [1951]
KONGRESS 1953 (Bamberg)	*Bericht über den Internationalen Musikwissenschaftlichen Kongress Bamberg 1953,* ed. by W. Brennecke, W. Kahl, and R. Steglich. Kassel: Bärenreiter-Verlag, 1954
KONGRESS 1958 (Cologne)	*Bericht über den siebenten Internationalen Musikwissenschaftlichen Kongress Köln 1958,* ed. by G. Abraham, S. Clercx-Lejeune, H. Federhofer, and W. Pfannkuch.* Kassel: Bärenreiter, 1959
KONGRESS 1960 (Chopin)	*The Book of the First International Musicological Congress Devoted to the Works of Frederick Chopin Warszawa 16th–22nd February, 1960.* Warsaw: Polish Scientific Publishers, 1963
KONGRESS 1961 (New York)	*Report of the Eighth Congress New York 1961,* ed. by J. LaRue, Vol. I. Kassel: Bärenreiter, 1961
KONGRESS 1962 (Kassel)	*Bericht über den Internationalen Musikwissenschaftlichen Kongress. Kassel 1962,* ed. by G. Reichert and M. Just. Kassel: Bärenreiter, 1963

Mf	Die Musikforschung
MfM	Monatshefte für Musikgeschichte
MGG	Die Musik in Geschichte und Gegenwart
Mk	Die Musik
ML	Music and Letters
MMB	Monumenta Musicae Belgicae
Mm	Le Mercure Musical
MMR	Monthly Musical Record
Mozart Jb	Mozart-Jahrbuch
MQ	Musical Quarterly
MR	The Music Review
ms	manuscript
MT	The Musical Times
MuK	Musik und Kirche
MWb	Musikalisches Wochenblatt
NA	Neue Ausgabe
Nagel	Nagels Musik-Archiv
Neues Beethoven Jb	Neues Beethoven-Jahrbuch
Neues Mozart Jb	Neues Mozart-Jahrbuch
n.d.	no date
n.p.	no publisher
NRMI	Nuova Rivista Musicale Italiana
NYPL	New York Public Library
NZfM	Neue Zeitschrift für Musik
OEE	Old English Edition
Österr MZ	Österreichishe Musikzeitschrift
PIMG	Publikationen der Internationalen Musikgesellschaft
PRMA	Proceedings of the Royal Musical Association
PSFM	Publications de la Société française de Musicologie
RaM	Rassegna Musicale
RB	Revue Belge de Musicologie
RM	Revue Musicale
RMI	Rivista Musicale Italiana
RMl	Revue de Musicologie
SIMG	Sammelbände der Internationalen Musikgesellschaft
SMl	Studia Musicologica
SMZ	Schweizerische Musikzeitung
StMw	Studien zur Musikwissenschaft (Beihefte der DTÖ)
supp.	supplement
trans.	translated, translator
VfMw	Vierteljahrsschrift für Musikwissenschaft

VogelB	Vogel, E. *Bibliothek der gedruckten weltlichen Vokalmusik in Italien aus den Jahren 1500–1700*
ZfM	Zeitschrift für Musik
ZfMw	Zeitschrift für Musikwissenschaft
ZIMG	Zeitschrift der Internationalen Musikgesellschaft

performance practice:

a bibliography

A

1 Abbado, Michelangelo. "La 'scordatura' negli strumenti ad arco e Nicolò Paganini," RaM XIII (1940) 213–26 (quotes from Praetorius, Marini, Biber, *et al.* and discusses scordatura in Paganini).

1.01 Aber, Adolf. "The Basso Continuo," MT LXXXIX (1948) 367–68.

1.02 ——. "On the Continuo in Bach," MT LXXXIX (1948) 169–71.

2 Adam, Louis. *Méthode de Piano du Conservatoire.* Paris: Au Magasin de Musique, 1804 (fingering, ornamentation, rhythm, tempo, pedaling).

3 ——. *Méthode Nouvelle pour le Piano.* Paris: 1802.

4 —— and Ludwig Lachnith. Introduction to *Méthode ou Principe Général du Doigté Pour Le Forte-Piano.* Paris: Sieber, [1798?] (fingering, touch, pedaling).

5 Adam, Wolfgang. "Zur Besetzung des Bach-Orchesters," Mk XII/1 (1912–13) 163–66.

5.01 Adams, James B. *A Familiar Introduction to the First Principles of Music. . . .* London: Printed for the author, [178–?] (incl. ornamentation).

6 Adler, Guido. "Das obligate Akkompagnement der Wiener Klassischen Schule," KONGRESS 1925 (Leipzig) 35–43 (texture).

7 —— (ed.). Preface to Heinrich Franz Biber's *Acht Violinsonaten,* DTÖ XI (Biber's "scordatura" from *Harmonia Artificiosa-Ariosa*).

7.01 —— (ed.). Preface to Johann Jakob Froberger's *Suiten für Klavier.* DTÖ XIII (tempo).

8 Adlung, Jakob. *Anleitung zu der musikalischen Gelahrtheit.* Erfurt: Druck und Verlag J. D. Jungnicol, 1758 (2nd ed. by J. A. Hiller. Dresden: Breitkopf, 1783). Fac. ed. by H. J. Moser. Kassel: Bärenreiter-Verlag, 1953 (*b. c.,* techniques [organ, clavier, voice], registration).

9 ——. *Musica Mechanica organoedi,* ed. by J. L. Albrecht, 2 vols. Berlin: Friedrich Wilhelm Birnstiel, 1768. Fac. ed. by C. Mahrenholz. Kassel: Bärenreiter-Verlag, 1961 (incl. registration).

10 Adrio, Adam. "Tobias Michaels Musicalische Seelenlust (1634/1637)," *Festschrift Helmuth Osthoff zum 65. Geburtstage,* ed. by L. Hoffmann-Erbrecht and H. Hucke. Tutzing: H. Schneider, 1961, 115–28 (treatise commentary, setting, instrumentation).

11 *Advice to the Composers and Performers of Vocal Musick. Translated from the Italian.* London: 1727.

12 Agazzari, Agostino. *Del sonare sopra'l basso con tvtti li stromenti e dell' vso loro nel conserto.* Siena: D. Falcini, 1607. Fac. ed. Milan: Bollettino bibliografico musical, 1933.

15

13 Agey, C. Buell (ed.). Preface to George F. Handel's *St. John Passion*. New York: Abingdon Press, 1963 (incl. tessitura, recitative, orchestra, *b. c.*).

13.01 Agricola, Martin. *Musica Choralis Deudsch*. Wittenberg: Georgen Rhaw, 1533 (mensural music).

13.02 ——. *Musica figuralis Deudsch*. Wittenberg: Georgen Rhaw, 1532 (rhythm, tempo).

14 ——. *Musica instrumentalis deudsch*. . . . Wittenberg: G. Rhaw, 1529. Partial fac. of 1529 and 1545 ed. by R. Eitner. Leipzig: Breitkopf & Härtel, 1896 (setting).

14.01 ——. *Rvdimenta mvsices, qvibvs canendi artificiva*, . . . Wittenberg: Georgen Rhaw, 1539 (incl. accidentals, forbidden intervals).

15 Ahlgrimm, Isolde and Erich Fiala. "Zur Aufführungspraxis der Bach-'schen Cembalowerke," Österr MZ IX (1954) 71–77 (implicit harpsichord techniques).

15.01 Aiguino, Illuminato. *Il tresoro illvminato di tvtti i tvoni di canto figurato* . . . . Venice: Appresso Giovanni Varisco, 1581 (esp. rhythm in mensural music).

16 Aitken, John. *A Compilation of the Litanies and Vespers Hymns and Anthems as they are sung in the Catholic Church*. Philadelphia: published by author, 1787. Reprint Philadelphia: Musical Americana, 1954 (ornaments, tempo).

16.01 Alain, Marie-Claire. "Appunti sulla 'Maniera Francese,'" *L'Organo* V (1964) 6–19 (*notes inégales*).

17 Albrecht, Hans. "Die Aufführungspraxis der italienischen Musik des 14. Jahrhunderts," unpublished Ph.D. diss., Berlin, 1925.

17.01 —— (ed.). *Die Bedeutung der Zeichen Keil, Strich und Punkt bei Mozart*. Kassel: Bärenreiter, 1957.

18 Albrechtsberger, Johann Georg. *Generalbass-Schule*. New ed. Leipzig: Hoffmeister and Kühnel, [1804].

18.01 ——. *Kurzgefasste Methode den Generalbass zu erlernen*. Vienna: Artaria, 1792.

19 Aldrich, Putnam. "The 'Authentic' Performance of Baroque Music," *Festschrift* DAVISON 161–71.

20 ——. "Bach's Technique of Transcription and Improvised Ornamentation," MQ XXXV (1949) 26–35.

21 ——. "Bachs Verzierungen insbesondere in seinen Orgelwerken," MuK XXVI (1956) 51–60.

22 ——. "Obligatory Improvisation of Ornaments," KONGRESS 1958 (Cologne) 55–56.

22.01 ——. "On the Interpretation of Bach's Trills," MQ XLIX (1963) 289–310.

23 ——. *Ornamentation in J. S. Bach's Organ Works*. New York: Coleman-Ross, 1950.

24 ——. "The principal *agréments* of the Seventeenth and Eighteenth

Centuries . . .," unpublished Ph.D. diss., Harvard University, 1942.

25 ——. *Rhythm in Seventeenth-Century Italian Monody.* New York: W. W. Norton, 1966.

26 d'Alembert, Jean Lerond. *Élémens de musique théorique et pratique . . .,* rev. ed. Lyon: Jean-Marie Bruyset, 1762 (incl. temperament, *b. c.*).

26.01 Algarotti, Francesco. *Saggio sopra l'opera in musica. . . .* Livorno: M. Coltellini, 1763 (1st ed. 1755). Eng. trans. as *An Essay on the Opera. Written in Italian by Count Algarotti.* Glasgow: R. Urie, 1768 (incl. recitative, singing, dances, scenery, glossary).

26.02 Allerup, Albert. *Die Musica practica des Johann Andreas Herbst und ihre entwicklungsgeschichtliche Bedeutung.* Kassel: Bärenreiter, 1931 (incl. ornamentation).

27 Altenburg, Johann Ernst. "On Clarin Playing and its Requirements," Chapter XI; and "On the Composing and Scoring of Trumpet Pieces," Chapter XII, from *An Essay on the Instruction of the Noble and Musical Art of Trumpet and Kettledrum Playing . . .,* trans. by M. Rasmussen, BQ II (1958–59) 20–30 (timbre, articulation).

28 ——. "On the Heroic Feldstücken, Principal- and Tafelblasen, and the So-Called Tonguing and Huffing (Haue)," Chapter X from *An Essay on the Instruction of the Noble and Musical Art of Trumpet and Kettledrum Playing . . .,* trans. by M. Rasmussen, BQ I (1957–58) 207–13 (tonguing).

29 ——. "On the Mouthpiece, Shanks or Tuning Buts, Crooks and Mutes," Chapter IX from *An Essay on the Instruction of the Noble and Musical Art of Trumpet and Kettledrum Playing . . .,* trans. by M. Rasmussen, BQ I (1957–58) 201–207 (uses of mutes, crooks, mouthpieces, and tuning techniques).

30 ——. "On the Trumpet Notes, Intervals, and their Relations," Chapter VIII from *An Essay on the Instruction of the Noble and Musical Art of Trumpet and Kettledrum Playing . . .,* Part Two "Practical Instructions for Learning the Trumpets and Kettledrums," trans. by M. Rasmussen, BQ I (1957–58) 133–45 (timbre, intonation).

31 ——. "On the Trumpet-Ornaments (Manieren)," Chapter XIII, and "On the Qualifications and Duties of Teacher and Student," Chapter XIV from *An Essay on the Instruction of the Noble and Musical Art of Trumpet and Kettledrum Playing . . .,* trans. by M. Rasmussen, BQ II (1957–58) 53–62 (ornaments).

32 Amann, Julius. *Allegris Miserere und die Aufführungspraxis in der Sixtina nach Reiseberichten und Musikhandschriften.* Regensburg: Pustet, 1935 (with extensive bibliography of Allegri's *Miserere*).

32.001 [Amat, Juan Carles]. *Guitarra espanola.* Valencia: Viuda de Agustin Laborda, 1639.

17

32.002 Ammerbach, Elias Nicolaus. *Orgel oder Instrument Tabulatur.* . . . Leipzig: [the author], 1571.

32.003 Andrea di Modena [Guicciardi?]. *Canto Harmonico.* . . . Modena: Eredi Cassiani Stampatori Episcopali, 1690 (comprehensive, indexed).

32.01 Andrews, H. K. "Transposition of Byrd's Vocal Polyphony," ML XLIII (1962) 25–37.

33 [Andrieu, J. F.?] *Kurtze Anführung zum General-Bass.* . . . 2nd ed. Leipzig: Augustus Martini, 1733 (cf. Mizler [von Kolof], *Anfangs-Gründe* . . .).

34 d'Anglebert, Jean-Henri. Preface to *Pièces de Clavecin*, PSFM Ser. 1 Vol. VIII, and *Le Trésor des Pianistes* XIX.

34.01 Apfel, Ernst. "Zur Frage des Rhythmus in der italienischen Monodie des 17. Jahrhunderts," Mf XXI (1968) 473–81.

35 Appia, Edmond. "The Aesthetics of Ornamentation in French Classical Music," *The Score* I (1949) 21–27 (d'Anglebert's ornaments).

36 ———. "Esthétique des 'Agréments' dans la musique française classique," SMZ LXXXIX (1949) 409–13.

36.01 Aprile, Guiseppe. *The Modern Italian Method of Singing.* . . . London: Rt. Birchall, [1795?] (1st pub. London: Broderip, 1791) (incl. written-out ornaments).

37 Arger, Jane. *Les agréments et le rythme.* Paris: Rouart, Lerolle, et Cie., [1921] (effect of ornamentation on tempo in vocal music).

38 ———. "La role expressif des 'Agréments' dans l'École vocale française de 1680 à 1760," RMl (1917–1919) 215–26.

39 Arkwright, Godfrey E. P. (ed.). Preface to Dr. John Blow's *Six Songs Selected from the Amphion Anglicus, 1700*, OEE XXIII (dotted rhythms).

40 —— (ed.). Preface to John Blow's *Venus and Adonis*, OEE XXV (ornamentation).

41 —— (ed.). Preface to John Milton's *Six Anthems*, OEE XXII (instrumental accompaniment).

42 —— (ed.). Preface to Henry Purcell's *Six Songs Selected from the Orpheus Brittanicus*, OEE XXIV (tempo).

42.01 Armitage-Smith, Julian. "Schubert's Appoggiaturas," MT CIII (1962) 534–36.

43 *Armonici erudimenti nei quali si contenzono le regole e suoi esempi per imparare accompagnare sul cimbalo il basso continovo.* . . . Florence: Nella stamperia di A. G. Pagani, e comp., 1790.

43.01 Arnold, Denis. " 'L'Incoronazione di Poppea' and its Orchestral Requirements," MT CIV (1963) 176–78.

44 ———. "The Influence of Ornamentation on the Structure of Early 17th Century Church Music," KONGRESS 1958 (Cologne) 57–58.

44.01 ———. "Instruments in Church: Some Facts and Figures," MMR LXXXV (1955) 32–38 (16th century).

45 —— (ed.). Preface to Giovanni Gabrieli's *Opera Omnia, Vol. I, Motetta, Concerti (1587), Sacrae Symphonae (1597)*. Rome: American Institute of Musicology, 1956 (text accentuation, orchestration).

46 Arnold, Frank T. *The Art of Accompaniment from a Thorough-Bass as Practised in the XVIIth and XVIIIth Centuries*. London: Oxford University Press, 1931.

47 Aubry, Pierre. "Estampies et Danses Royales ...," Mm III (1906) 169–201 (instrumentation).

48 ——. "La Musique et les Musiciens d'Église en Normandie aux XIII⁰ Siècle d'après le 'Journal des visites pastorales' d'Odon Rigaud," Mm II (1906) 337–47, 455–62, 505–12, 556–68; III (1907) 17–26, 58–63 (singing).

49 Auda, Antoine. "Le 'Tactus' dans la Messe 'L'homme armé' de Palestrina," AMl XIV (1942) 27–67.

50 Auerbach, Cornelia. *Die deutsche Clavichordkunst des 18. Jahrhunderts*. Kassel: Bärenreiter-Verlag, 1930 (incl. question of cembalo, clavichord, or piano).

51 Aulabaugh, Alan Richard. "An Analytical Study of Performance Problems in the Keyboard Sonatas of F. J. Haydn," unpublished Ph.D. diss., State University of Iowa, 1958 (rhythm, ornamentation, dynamics).

52 Avison, Charles. *An Essay on Musical Expression*. London: C. Davis, 1752 (cf. 2nd ed. of 1753 for Avison's "Reply" to Wm. Hayes' "Remarks on the 'Essay on Musical Expression'").

53 Azzoni, Giulio and Giovanni Tebaldini. "Interpreti ed interpretazioni della musica di G. S. Bach: Studio critico d'indagine con citazioni ed esempi musicali da Czerny a Busoni," RMI XLIX (1947) 25–45.

B

54 Babitz, Sol. "Concerning the Length of Time that Every Note must be Held," MR XXVIII (1967) 21–37 (*notes inégales*).

55 ——. "Differences Between 18th-Century and Modern Violin Bowing," *The Score* 19 (1957) 34–55 (quotes Geminiani, L. Mozart, and Quantz).

55.01 ——. "Modern Errors in Mozart Performance," Mozart Jb (1967) 62–89. With additions and corrections as of May 1969, incl. remarks on Beethoven performance. (Early Music Laboratory Bulletin 5). Los Angeles: Early Music Laboratory, 1969. (Rubato, tone production, articulation, bowing, metric accent, dynamics, fingering, instruments, tempo and technique).

55.02 ——. "On Using Early Keyboard Fingering," (Early Music Laboratory Bulletin 3). Revised and enlarged reprinting of articles which appeared in Feb., March, and April 1969, issues

19

of *The Diapason*. Los Angeles: Early Music Laboratory, 1969 (J. S. and C. P. E. Bach, Couperin, Ammerbach, Quantz, Sancta Maria, Mozart; esp. *notes inégales*).

56 ——. "On Using J. S. Bach's Keyboard Fingerings," ML XLIII (1962) 123–28 (incl. *notes inégales*, fingerings, ornamentation).

57 ——. "A Problem of Rhythm in Baroque Music," MQ XXXVIII (1952) 533–65 (*notes inégales*).

58 ——. "The Vega Bach Bow: A Reply to Dr. Emil Telmányi," MT XCVI (1955) 251–53 (cf. Stevens, "Another view . . .," Telmányi, "Lösung . . .," "Purpose . . .," "Some problems . . .").

59 ——, John Byrt, and Michael Collins. "Three Further Views on *Notes Inégales*," JAMS XX (1967) 473–85.

60 Bach, Johann Michael. *Kurze und systematische Anleitung zum General-Bass*. . . . Cassel: Gedruckt in der Waysenhaus-Buchdruckerey, 1780.

61 Bach, Karl Philipp Emanuel. *Versuch über die wahre Art das Clavier zu spielen*. Berlin: In vorlegung des Auctoris, 1759 and 1762. Facs. of Pts. I and II ed. by L. Hoffmann-Erbrecht. Leipzig: C. F. Kahnt, 1957. Trans. and ed. by W. J. Mitchell as *Essay on the True Art of Playing Keyboard Instruments*. New York: W. W. Norton, 1949 (incl. ornaments, *b. c.*, accompaniment, improvisation).

61.01 Bacher, Joseph. *Die Viola da Gamba*. Kassel: Bärenreiter, [1932] (incl. method, based on historical sources).

62 Bacilly, Bénigne de. *Remarques curieuses sur l'art de bien chanter*. Paris: C. Blageart, 1668 (cf. Caswell, "Development . . .").

63 Bacon, Richard Mackenzie. *Elements of Vocal Science*. . . . London: Baldwin, Cradock & Joy, [1824]. Ed. by E. Foreman. Champaign: Pro Musica Press, 1968.

64 Badura-Skoda, Eva. "Über die Anbringungen von Auszierungen in den Klavierwerken Mozarts," Mozart Jb (1957) 186–98.

65 Badura-Skoda, Eva and Paul. *Interpreting Mozart on the Keyboard*, trans. by L. Black. London: Barrie and Rockliff, 1962 (incl. embellishment).

66 Badura-Skoda, Paul. "Über das Generalbass-Spiel in den Klavier-Konzerten Mozarts," Mozart Jb (1957) 96–107.

67 ——. "Über Mozarts Tempi," Österr MZ IX (1954) 347–51 (incl. Mozart's own statements).

68 Bär, Carl. "Zum Begriff des 'Basso' in Mozarts Serenaden," Mozart Jb (1960–61) 133–55.

69 [Baillie, Alexander?]. *An Introduction to the Knowledge and Practice of the Thoro'bass*. Edinburgh: [n. p.], 1717.

70 Baillot, Pierre Marie François de Sales. *L'art du violon*. Paris: au Depot Central de la Musique, [n. d.] (19th century).

71 Baillot, Pierre Marie François de Sales, Rudolphe Kreutzer, and Pierre Rode. *Méthode de violon.* Paris: Au Magasin de Musique, [1802]. Eng. trans. as *The Celebrated Method for the Violin.* Philadelphia: G. E. Blake, [18—] (incl. graces, ornamentation, bowing, tone).

71.01 Banchieri, Adriano. *Cartella musicale nel canto figurato, fermo et contrapunto.* Venice: Giacomo Vincenti, 1614 (incl. vocal embellishment).

71.02 ———. *Organo Svonarino.* . . . Venice: Appresso Alessandro Vincenti, 1638.

72 ———. Preface to *La Pazzia Senile (1601),* VogelB I 56–57 (incl. description of performance).

73 Barbé, Henriette. "Die Ausführung von Vorschlägen im Barock, insbesondere bei J. S. Bach," SMZ CIV (1964) 346–52.

74 Barblan, Guglielmo. "Le orchestre in Lombardia all'epoca di Mozart," *Bericht über den Internationalen Musikwissenschaftlichen Kongress Wien Mozartjahr 1956 3. bis 9. Juni,* ed. E. Schenk. Graz-Cologne: Verlag Hermann Böhlaus Nachf., 1958 18–21 (size of orchestras at Mantova, Cremona, Milan).

75 Barbour, J. Murray. "Bach and 'The Art of Temperament,'" MQ XXXIII (1947) 64–89.

76 ———. *Tuning and Temperament.* . . . East Lansing: Michigan State College Press, 1951.

76.01 Barker, E. Phillips. "Master Thoinot's Fancy," ML XI (1930) 383–93 (Arbeau's *L'Orchésographie*).

76.011 Barnes, Clifford. "Vocal Music at the 'Théâtres de la Foire' 1697–1762," *Recherches sur la Musique Française Classique* VIII (1968) 141–60 (vocal style in *opéra-comique*).

76.02 Barnett, Dene. "Music and Dancing in the Grand Siècle," *Canon* XVII/1 (1964) 15–25 (violin).

77 Baron, Ernst Gottlieb. *Historisch-theoretisch und practische Untersuchung des Instruments der Lauten.* . . . Nuremberg: J. F. Rüdiger, 1727 (incl. *b. c.*).

78 Barthélemy, Maurice. "L'orchestre et l'orchestration des œuvres de Campra," RM No. 226 (1955) 97–104 (size, settings).

79 Bassani, Giovanni. *Motetti, Madrigali et Canzoni francese . . . diminuiti per sonar con ogni sorte di stromenti . . . .* Venice: 1591.

80 ———. *Ricercate, Passaggi et Cadentie, per potersi essercitar nel diminuir. . . .* Venice: 1585.

81 Bathe, William. *A Briefe Introduction to the Skill of Song.* London: [?1590].

82 Baud-Bovy, Samuel. "L'interprétation rythmique des Ouvertures pour orchestre de J. S. Bach," SMZ LXXXIV (1944) 181–84.

83 Baum, Günther. "Die Rezitativschlüsse der Matthäus-Passion," *Musica* IV (1950) 265–69 (rhythm and tempo, fermatas).

84 Bayer, Friedrich. "Über den Gebrauch der Instrumente in den Kirchen- und Instrumentalwerken von Wolfgang Amadeus Mozart," StMw XIV (1927) 33–74 (choral and orchestral).

84.01 Bayly, Anselm. *A Practical Treatise on Singing and Playing.* . . . London: J. Ridley, 1771 (based on Tosi).

85 Beck, Hermann. "Bemerkungen zu Beethovens Tempi," Beethoven Jb II (1955–56) 24–54 (cf. *infra*).

86 ——. "Das Soloinstrument im Tutti des Konzerts der zweiten Hälfte des 18. Jahrhunderts," Mf XIV (1961) 427–35 (incl. *b. c.*).

87 ——. "Studien über das Tempoproblem bei Beethoven," unpublished Ph.D. diss., Erlangen, 1954 (cf. *supra*).

88 Beck, Sydney (ed.). Introduction to Thomas Morley's *First Book of Consort Lessons, 1599 & 1611.* New York: C. F. Peters, 1959 (instrumentation, improvisation, ornamentation).

89 Beckmann, Gustav. *Das Violinspiel in Deutschland vor 1700.* Leipzig: Simrock, 1918 (incl. diminution, scordatura, fingering).

90 Beer, R. "Ornaments in Old Keyboard Music," MR XIII (1952) 3–13.

91 [Beethoven, Ludwig van]. *Studien im Generalbasse, Contrapuncte und in der Compositions-Lehre,* coll. and ed. by I. R. von Seyfried. Vienna: Verlag von Tobias Haslinger, [1832]. Eng. trans. by H. H. Pierson as *Studies in Thorough-Bass, Counterpoint and the Art of Scientific Composition.* Leipzig: Schubert & Co., 1853 (based on Albrechtsberger).

92 Bemetzrieder, Anton. *Leçons de clavecin, et principes d'harmonie.* Paris: Bluet, 1771 (incl. *b. c.*).

93 ——. *Music made Easy to every Capacity* . . ., trans. by G. Bernard. London: Birchall and Andrews, 1785 (incl. fingering, *b. c.*).

93.01 ——. *Nouvelles leçons de clavecin ou Instructions générales sur la musique vocale & instrumentale.* . . . London: Printed and sold by the author, 1783 (incl. *b. c.*, ornamentation).

94 Berard, Jean Antoine. *L'art du chant.* . . . Paris: Dessaint & Saillant, 1755 (incl. ornamentation, articulation).

94.01 Berbiguier, T. *Nouvelle Méthode pour la Flûte.* Paris: Janet et Cotelle, [n. d.].

95 Bergmann, Walter. "Some Old and New Problems of Playing the Basso Continuo," PRMA LXXXVII (1960–61) 31–43 (quotes Avison, Couperin).

95.01 Bergsagel, John. "On the Performance of Ludford's Alternatim Masses," *Musica Disciplina* XVI (1962) 35–55 (*accompanimenta cappella* vs. organ).

95.02 Berljawsky, Joseph. "The Evolution of the Vibrato," *The Strad* LXXVIII (1967) 255–62 (quotes theorists, incl. musical exx.).

96 Bermudo, Juan. . . . *Declaracion de instrumentos musicales.* Osuna: Juan de Leon, 1549 and 1555. Fac. ed. by M. S. Kastner. Kassel: Bärenreiter-Verlag, 1957 (vihuela, keyboard, singing, *et al.*).

96.01 Bertalotti, Angelo Michele. *Regole facilissime per apprendere con facilità* *e prestezza li Canti fermo, e figurato.* . . . Bologna: Per Marino Silvani, 1698 (rhythm, accidentals).

97 Besseler, Heinrich. "Sulla disposizione delle masse orchestrali e corali negli ambienti destinati alle esecuzioni profane e religiose nell'età barocca," KONGRESS 1938 (Florence) 121–27.

98 Béthisy, Jean-Laurent de. *Exposition de la théorie et de la pratique de la musique* . . ., 2nd ed. Paris: F. G. Deschamps, 1764 (incl. *b. c.*, temperament).

99 Beyschlag, Adolf. *Die Ornamentik der Musik.* Leipzig: Breitkopf & Härtel, 1908.

100 ——. "Über Chrysander's Bearbeitung des Händel'schen 'Messias' und über die Musikpraxis zur Zeit Händel's," Mk X/3 (1910–11) 143–58 (criticism of Chrysander).

101 ——. "Über Irrlehren in der Ornamentik der Musik," Mk XIII/1 (1913–14) 104–09 (Baroque to Romantic).

102 ——. "Über Vorschläge und andere Verzierungen," AMz XXVII (1900) 471–73, 487–89, 503–04, 519–20.

102.01 Bianchini, Francesco. *De tribus generibus instrumentorum musicae veterum organicae dissertatio.* Rome: Bernabò and Lazzarini, 1742.

103 Bianciardi, Francesco, *Breve regola per imparar' a sonare sopra il Basso.* . . . Siena: [n. p.], 1607.

104 Bicknell, Joan Colleen. "On performing Purcell's vocal Music: some neglected Evidence," MR XXV (1964) 27–33 (rhythm, tempo, ornamentation, *b. c.*).

104.01 Bird, Ruth Holmes (Scott). "Music among the Moravians, Bethlehem, Pennsylvania," unpublished M.M. thesis, Eastman School of Music, 1938 (use of the trombone choir).

104.02 *The Bird Fancyer's Delight.* . . . London: Richard Meares, 1717 (flageolet fingering and ornaments).

105 Birtner, Herbert. "Grundsätzliche Bemerkungen zur Schütz-Pflege in unserer Zeit," MuK VII (1935) 206–218 (*b. c.*).

106 Bixler, Martha. "An Introduction to Renaissance Ornamentation," AR VIII/4 (1967) 107–09 and IX/4 (1968) 108–12 (incl. realizations).

106.01 Blakely, Lloyd G. "Johann Conrad Beissel and Music of the Ephrata Cloister," JRME XV (1967) 120–38 (incl. trans. of preface to *Das Gesäng Der einsamen und verlassenen Turtel-Taube* . . . [1747]).

106.02 Blanchet, [Jean]. *L'art, ou les principes philosophiques du chant.* Paris: August. Mart. Lottin, 1756 (incl. ornamentation).

107 Blandford, W. F. H. "Bach's Trumpet," letter in MMR LXI (1931) 44–45.

108 ——. "Handel's Horn and Trombone Parts," MT LXXX (1939) 697–99, 746–47, 794.

109 Blankenburg, Quirinus van. *Elementa musica, of Nieuw licht tot het welver-*

23

staan van de musiec en de bas-continuo. . . . 's Gravenhage: L. Berkoske, 1739.

110 Blankenburg, Walter. "Besetzungsfrage in Bachs Werken—Von sonstigen Passionsaufführungen," MuK XXV (1955) 170–72.

111 ——. "Von der Verwendung von Blechblasinstrumenten in Bachs Kirchenmusikalischen Werke und ihrer Bedeutung," MuK XX (1950) 65–71.

112 ——. "Zur Aufführungspraxis und wiedergabe von Bach'schen Choralsätzen," MuK XXVI (1956) 19–23 (tempo, dynamics, fermatas).

112.01 Blewitt, Jonas. *A Complete Treatise on the Organ.* . . . *Op. 4.* London: Longman and Broderip, [17—?] (esp. registration [exx.]).

113 Blindow, Martin. "Eine Quelle zur Pedaltechnik des 18. Jahrhunderts," MuK XXVIII (1958) 127–29 (quotes Samuel Petri).

114 Blume, Friedrich. "Musikforschung und Musikpraxis," Festschrift STEIN 13–25.

115 Bodky, Erwin. "Das Cembalo-Clavichord Problem," Mk XXIV (1931) 97–101.

116 ——. *The Interpretation of Bach's Keyboard Works.* Cambridge: Harvard University Press, 1960.

117 ——. "New Contributions to the Problem of the Interpretation of Bach's Keyboard Works," *Report . . . International Musicological Society Fifth Congress Utrecht 1952.* Amsterdam: G. Alsbach, 1953 73–78.

117.01 Boetticher, Wolfgang. "Neue textkritische Forschungen an R. Schumanns Klavierwerk," AfMw XXV (1968) 46–76 (esp. Part II of the article).

118 ——. "Studien zur solistischen Lautenpraxis des 16. und 17. Jahrhunderts," unpublished Ph.D. diss., Berlin, 1943.

119 Bonaccorsi, Alfredo. "La dinamica nella storia," RaM XXVII (1957) 290–95 (according to Demantius, Praetorius, Zarlino, *et al.*).

120 ——. "Terminologia confusa: vibrato, tremolo, bebung," RaM XIX (1949) 52–53 (as used by B. Marini, Ganassi, Geminiani, *et al.*).

121 Bonisconti, Angiola Maria. "Il violinismo di Bach nella pratica moderna," RaM XX (1950) 244–49 (partitas and sonatas).

122 Bononcini, Giovanni Maria. *Musico prattico.* Bologna: Giacomo Monti, 1673 (*b. c.*).

122.01 Bonta, Stephen. "Liturgical Problems in Monteverdi's Marian Vespers," JAMS XX (1967) 87–106 (incl. instrumentation).

122.02 Borghese, Antoine D. R. *L'art musical ramené à ses vrais principes,* . . . Paris: Hardouin & Gattey, 1786 (incl. singing, *b. c.*).

122.03 [Borjon, Charles Emmanuel]. *Traité de la musette.* . . . Lyon: Jean Girin and Barthelemy Riviere, 1672.

123 Bornefeld, Helmut. "Instrumente in der Kirchenmusik," MuK XI (1939) 59–70.

124 Borrel, Eugène. "La basse chiffrée dans l'École française au XVIIIe siècle," RMl II (1920–1921) 66–70.

125 ———. *Contribution à l'interprétation de la musique française au XVIIIe siècle.* Paris: Bureau d'Éditions de la "Schola," 1916 (incl. ornaments, tempo).

126 ———. "Les indications métronomiques laissées par les auteurs français du XVIIIe siècle," RMl IX (1928) 149–53.

127 ———. "L'interprétation de l'ancien recitatif français," RMl XII (1931) 13–21 (rhythm).

128 ———. *L'interprétation de la musique française (de Lully à la Revolution).* Paris: au Bureau d'Édition de la "Schola," 1934.

129 ———. *La réalisation de la Basse Chiffrée dans les œuvres de l'École français au XVIIIe siècle.* Paris: Éditions de la "Schola," 1920.

130 ———. "Les notes inégales dans l'ancienne musique française," RMl XII (1931) 278–89.

131 ———. "Notes sur l'orchestration de l'opéra *Jephté* de Montéclair (1733), et de la Symphonie *les Élémens* de J.-F. Rebel (1737)," RM No. 226 (1955) 105–16 (specific indications).

132 ———. "Un cours d'interprétation de la musique de violon au XVIIIe siècle par Cambini," RMl X (1929) 120–24 (fingering).

133 Borroff, Edith (ed.). Preface to Jean-Joseph Cassanea de Mondonville's *Jubilate.* Pittsburgh: University of Pittsburgh Press, 1961 (ornaments, *b. c.*, instrumentation, tempo).

133.01 Bostrom, Marvin J. "Eighteenth Century Keyboard Instruction Practices as Revealed in a Set of Master Lessons," JRME XIII (1965) 33–38 (quotes M. Wiedeburg's *The Self-informing Clavier Player*).

134 Bottrigari, Hercole. *Il Desiderio* (1594), trans. by Carol MacClintock, [Rome]: American Institute of Musicology, 1962 (esp. instrumental) (cf. Giustiniani, *Discourso . . .*).

135 Boutmy, [Jean Baptiste Joseph?]. *Traité Abregé sur la Basse Continue . . .*, Fr.-Dutch ed. The Hague: B. Hummel, [1760?].

136 Bovicelli, Giovanni Battista. *Regole, passaggi di musica, madrigali, e motetti passeggiati. . . .* Venice: Giacomo Vincenti, 1594. Fac. ed. by N. Bridgeman. Kassel: Bärenreiter-Verlag, 1957.

137 Bowles, Edmund A. "La hiérarchie des instruments de musique dans l'Europe féodale," RMl XLII (1958) 155–69 (music proper to each instrument).

138 ———. "Musical Instruments at the Medieval Banquet," RB XII (1958) 41–51 (music proper to instrument and occasion).

138.01 ———. "Musical Instruments in the Medieval Corpus Christi Procession," JAMS XVII (1964) 251–60.

139 ———. "The Organ in the Medieval Liturgical Service," RB XVI (1962) 13–29 (when appropriate to use).

25

139.01 ——. "The Role of Musical Instruments in Medieval Sacred Drama," MQ XLV (1959) 67–84.

140 Bowman, Horace B. "A Study of the Castrati Singers and Their Music," unpublished Ph.D. diss., Indiana University, 1952.

141 Boyden, David D. "Ariosti's Lessons for Viola d'Amore," MQ XXXII (1946) 545–63.

142 ——. "Dynamics in Seventeenth- and Eighteenth-Century Music," Festschrift DAVISON 186–93 (evidence against terrace dynamics).

142.01 ——. "Geminiani and the First Violin Tutor." AMl XXXI (1959) 160–70 (incl. bibl. of 17–18th c. Eng. violin treatises) (cf. Geminiani, "The Art of Playing . . .").

143 ——. *The History of Violin Playing, from its Origins to 1761, and its Relationship to the Violin and Violin Music.* New York: Oxford University Press, 1965.

144 ——. "The Missing Manuscript of Tartini's 'Traité des Agrémens,'" MQ XLVI (1960) 315–28.

145 ——. "Monteverdi's Violini Piccoli alla Francese and Viole da Brazz'," AnnMl VI (1958) 387–401.

145.01 ——. "Prelleur, Geminiani, and Just Intonation," JAMS IV (1951) 202–19.

146 ——. "The Violin and its Technique in the 18th Century," MQ XXXVI (1950) 9–38 (ornaments, vibrato, bowing, articulation).

147 ——. "The Violin and its Technique: New Horizons in Research," KONGRESS 1958 (Cologne) 29–39.

148 Braun, Friedbert. "Studien zur Dynamik in Schuberts Instrumentalmusik," unpublished Ph.D. diss., Tübingen, 1960.

149 [Breakspear, Eustace J. ?]. "The Execution of the Ornamental 'Turn,'" MMR V (1875) 80–81 (Beethoven and Hummel).

149.001 Breig, Werner. "Scheidemanns Barocker Orgelstil und die Norddeutsche Schule," *Beihefte zum* AfMw III (1967) 101–05 (17th century).

149.01 Brenet, Michel. "French Military Music in the Reign of Louis XIV," MQ III (1917) 340–57 (esp. instrumentation, rhythm).

150 ——. "Notes sur l'introduction des instruments dans les églises de France," Festschrift REIMANN 277–86.

150.01 Brennecke, Ernest, Jr. *John Milton the Elder and his Music.* New York: Columbia University Press, 1938 (performance of English church and secular music near the end of the 16th century).

151 Bridgeman, Nanie. "G. C. Maffei et sa lettre sur le chant," RMl XXXVIII (1956) 3–34 (vocal ornamentation).

152 Britten, Benjamin. "On Realizing the Continuo in Purcell's Songs," *Henry Purcell 1659–1695: Essays on His Music*, ed. by I. Holst. London: Oxford University Press, 1959 7–13.

26

153 Broder, Nathan. "Mozart and the 'Clavier,'" MQ XXVII (1941) 422–32 (harpsichord or piano).

154 Brookbank [?]. *The Well-tuned Organ.* London: [n. p.], 1660 (instrumental music and/or accompaniment in church services).

154.01 Brossard, Sébastian de. *Dictionnaire de musique. . . .* Paris: C. Ballard, 1703 (incl. various references and exx. of ornamentation).

155 Bruck, Boris. "Wandlungen des Begriffes Tempo rubato," unpublished Ph.D. diss., Erlangen, 1928 (Romantic Era).

155.01 Bruinsma, Henry A. "The Organ Controversy in the Netherlands Reformation to 1640," JAMS VII (1954) 205–12 (when and if organ was used).

156 Brunner, Hans. *Das Klavierklangideal Mozarts und die Klaviere seiner Zeit.* Augsburg: Filser, 1933.

157 Brunold, Paul. *Traité des Signes et Agréments employés par les Clavecinistes Français des XVIIe et XVIIIe Siècles.* Lyon: Les Éditions musicales Janin, 1925.

158 Buchmayer, Richard. "Cembalo oder Pianoforte?" BJ V (1908) 64–94.

159 Buelow, George J. "The Full-voiced Style of Thorough-Bass Realization," AM1 XXXV (1963) 159–71 (18th century).

159.01 ——. *Thorough-Bass According to Johann David Heinichen.* Berkeley: University of California Press, 1966 (cf. Heinichen, "Der General-Bass. . . .").

160 Buhle, Edward. *Die musikalischen Instrumente in den Miniaturen des frühen Mittelalters: Ein Beitrag zur Geschichte der Musikinstrumente.* Leipzig: Breitkopf & Härtel, 1903 (incl. iconography).

160.01 Bukofzer, Manfred F. "On the Performance of Renaissance Music," *Proceedings of the Music Teachers National Association* Series 36 (1941) 225–35.

161 Bullivant, Roger. "Zum Problem der Begleitung der Bachschen Motetten," BJ LII (1966) 59–68.

162 Burman, Erik. . . . *Dissertatio musica, De basso fundamenti.* . . . Uppsala: literis Wernerianis [1728].

163 Burney, Charles. *An Account of the Musical Performances in Westminster Abbey and the Pantheon in Commemoration of Handel.* London: T. Payne, 1785. Fac. ed., Amsterdam: Frits A. M. Knuf, 1964.

164 Burrowes, John F. *The Thorough-Base Primer.* . . . London: for the author by Clementi and Co., 1819.

165 Butler, Charles. *The Principles of Musik, in Singing and Setting.* London: J. Haviland, 1636.

C

166 Caccini, Giulio. Preface to *L'Euridice (1600)*, VogelB I 123–24 (monody).

167 ——. Preface to *Le Nuove Musiche* (*1601*), VogelB I 125–26 (monody).

168 ——. Preface to *Nuove Musiche e Nuova Maniera di Scriverle* (*1614*), VogelB I 128–29 (monody).

169 Cahn-Speyer, Rudolf. "Über einige typische Fehler bei der Inszenierung älterer Opern," Mk XI/3 (1911–12) 79–87 (Classic and early Romantic).

170 ——. "Über historisch korrekte Aufführungen älterer Musik," Mk XI/1 (1911–12) 204–21.

171 Callenberg, Eitel-Friedrich. "Das obersächsische Barocklied. Wort und Ton in der Musiklehre des 17. Jahrhunderts," unpublished Ph.D. diss., Freiburg, 1952.

171.01 Calvocoressi, Michael D. "The Genuine Scoring of Mussorgsky's 'Boris Godunov,'" MMR LVIII (1928) 328, 359.

172 Caporali, Rodolfo. "La scrittura pianistica chopiniana e la sua interpretazione," RaM XIX (1949) 286–95 (esp. Opus 10).

173 Carapetyan, Armen (ed.). Preface to Antonii Brumel's *Missa L'Homme Armé*. Rome: American Institute of Musicology, 1951 (tactus, accidentals).

173.001 Carissimi, Giovanni Giacomo. *Ars cantandi.* . . . Augsburg: J. Koppmayer, 1693. Trans. by J. R. Douglas as "The Art of Singing; A Translation in English of 'Ars Cantandi'; From an edition of 1693 of a German translation of the original in Italian by Giovanni Giacomo Carissimi," unpublished M.S.M. thesis, Union Theological Seminary, 1949 (incl. rhythm, tempo).

173.002 Carpe, Adolph. *Der Rhythmus: Sein Wesen in der Kunst und seine Bedeutung im musikalischen Vortrage*. Leipzig: Gebrüder Reinecke, [n. d.] (esp. Chopin, Schumann).

173.003 Carpenter, Hoyle. "Tempo and Tactus in the Age of Cabezón," AnM XXI (1966) 123–30.

173.01 Carse, Adam von Ahn. "Brass Instruments in the Orchestra," ML III (1922) 378–82 (when used before 1800).

173.02 ——. "Fingering the Recorder," MR I (1940) 96–104 (esp. chromatic fingerings before 1800).

174 ——. *The History of Orchestration*. London: Kegan Paul, Trench, Trubner & Co., Ltd., 1925 (incl. instrumentation and orchestration, sonorities, conducting).

175 ——. *The Orchestra in the XVIIIth Century*. Cambridge: W. Heffer and Sons, Ltd., 1940 (conducting, doubling of parts, availability cf scores).

175.01 ——. "XVII Century Orchestral Instruments," ML I (1920) 334–42 (instrumentation).

176 Cartier, Jean-Baptiste. *L'art du violon*. Paris: Decombe, 1798 (incl. ornamentation of slow movements).

177 Carulli, Ferdinando. *Méthode Complète pour parvenir à pincer de la Guitare* . . . , 5th ed. Paris: Carli, 1810 (incl. ornamentation).

178 Casey, William Sherman. "Printed English Lute Instruction Books, 1568–1610," unpublished Ph.D. diss., University of Michigan, 1960 (technique, tablature, transcriptions).

179 Caswell, Austin B., Jr. "The Development of Seventeenth-Century French Vocal Ornamentation and Its Influence upon Late Baroque Ornamentation Practice," unpublished Ph.D. diss., University of Minnesota, 1964 (cf. Bacilly, *Remarques* . . .).

179.01 Caux de Cappeval, N. de. *Apologie du goût françois, relativement à l'opéra: poème*. Paris: [n. p.], 1754 (French and Italian opera).

180 Cavalieri, Emilio del. Preface to *Rappresentatione di Anima et di Corpo*, VogelB I 150–53 (monody).

180.01 Cavanaugh, Robert (ed.). Preface to Thomas Tomkins' *Thirteen Anthems*. New Haven: A–R Editions, 1968 (accompaniment, pitch, tempo).

181 [Cazotte, Jacques]. *Observations sur la lettre de J. J. Rousseau, au sujet de la musique française*. Paris: [n. p.] 1754 (opera).

181.01 Celletti, Rodolfo. "Origine e sviluppi della Coloratura Rossiniana," NRMI V (1968) 872–919 (vocal embellishments in Rossini).

182 Cellier, Alex (ed.). Preface to Michel-Richard de Lalande's *De Profundis*. Paris: Rouart, Lerolle, et Cie, 1944 (incl. ornamentation, instruments).

183 —— (ed.). Preface to Michel-Richard de Lalande's *Quare Fremuerunt Gentes*. Paris: Rouart, Lerolle et Cie, 1949 (division of orchestra into choirs, tempo, ornamentation).

184 Cerone, Domenico Pietro. *El melopeo y maestro*. Naples: Gargano & Nucci, 1613 (incl. ornamentation, improvisation, instrumentation).

185 Cerreto, Scipione. *Dell' arbore musicale, espositioni dodici*. Naples: Giov. B. Sottile, Scipione Bonino, 1608.

186 Cesari, Gaetano. "Tre tavole di strumenti in un 'Boezio' del X secolo," Festschrift ADLER 26–28 (iconography).

187 Chailley, Jacques (ed.). Preface to Guillaume de Machaut's *Messe Notre Dame*. Paris: Éditions Salabert, 1948 (incl. tessitura, instrumentation).

187.01 Chambonnières, Jacques Champion. Preface to *Pièces de clavecin, 1ᵉʳ Livre*. Paris: chez Jollain, 1670. In *Oeuvres complètes de Chambonnières*, ed. by Brunold & Tessier. Paris: Editions Maurice Senart, [1925] (incl. table of ornaments).

187.02 Charnassé, Hélène. "Sur l'Accord de la Guitare," *Recherches sur la Musique Française Classique* VII (1967) 25–37 (guitar tuning, 16th-18th centuries).

188 Chatwin, R. B. "Handel and the Clarinet," GSJ III (1950) 3–8.

189 Chechlińska, Zofia. "Das Problem der Form und die Reelle Klanggestalt in Chopin's Präludien," KONGRESS 1960 (Chopin) 425–29 (incl. tempo, dynamics).

29

190 Cherbuliez, Antoine-Elisée. "Graviseth's *Heulelia* (1658) über die musikalische Aufführungspraxis in der Schweiz," *Mitteilungen der Schweiz Musikforschenden Gesellschaft* I (1934) 14–15, 25–32.

190.01 Ching, James. "On the Playing of Bach's Clavier Music," MT XCI (1950) 299–301.

191 Chiodino, Giovanni Battista. *Arte prattica & poëtica*. . . . Frankfurt: A. Hummen, in verlegung/T. M. Götzens, 1653.

192 Christmann, Arthur H. "Johann Joachim Quantz on the Musical Practices of His Time," unpublished Ph.D. diss., Union Theological Seminary, 1950.

193 Chrysander, Friedrich. "Die Originalstimmen zu Händels Messias," JbP II (1895) 11–19 (instrumentation).

194 ——. "Lodovico Zacconi als Lehrer des Kunstgesanges," VfMw IX (1893) 249–310, X (1894) 531–67 (early Baroque vocal technique and ornamentation, Zacconi's *Prattica* I and II).

195 Chybiński, Adolf. *Beiträge zur Geschichte des Taktschlagens*. Leipzig: Breitkopf & Härtel, 1912.

196 ——. "Zur Geschichte des Taktschlagens und des Kapellmeisteramtes in der Epoche der Mensuralmusik," SIMG X (1908–09) 385–95. (Renaissance, conducting) (cf. Schünemann, "Zur Frage . . .").

196.01 Clarkson, Frank A. "The Violin in the Nineteenth Century," *The Strad* LXXIX (1968) 141–47 (violin technique, esp. vibrato and bowing).

196.02 ——. "Violin Technique in the Seventeenth Century," *The Strad* LXXVII (1967) 332–37 (incl. instrumentation, bowing).

197 Clément, Charles François. *Essai sur l'accompagnement du clavecin*. . . . Paris: C. Ballard, 1758.

197.01 Clementi, Muzio. *Introduction to the Art of Playing on the Pianoforte*. . . . London: Clementi, Banger, Hyde, Collard & Davis, [180–] (incl. fingering, ornamentation, 18th-century exx.).

198 Closson, Ernest (ed.). *Le Manuscript dit des Basses Danses de la Bibliothèque de Bourgogne*. [Brussels]: Société des Bibliophiles et Iconophiles de Belgique, 1912 (instrumentation).

199 Coar, Birchard. *The Masters of the Classical Period as Conductors*. Dekalb: Private Printing, 1949 (from Bach to Beethoven).

199.01 Coates, Henry (ed.). *The Bach Technique of Organ Pedalling as Shown in His Organ Works*. London: Edwin Ashdown Ltd., 1953.

200 Coclico, Adrianus Petit. *Compendium musices descriptum*. Nuremberg: I. Berg & V. Neuber, 1552. Fac. ed. by M. F. Bukofzer. Kassel: Bärenreiter-Verlag, 1954.

200.001 Codingnola, Arturo. *Paganini intimo*. Genova: Edito a Cura Del Municipo di Genova, 1935 (contemporary descriptions of Paganini's playing).

200.01 Cole, Frances Elaine. "Bach's 'Goldberg Variations': A Descriptive

Study and Analysis," unpublished Ed. D. diss., Teachers College, Columbia University, 1966 (esp. Chapter IV).

201 Collins, Michael B. "The Performance of Coloration, Sesquialtera, and Hemiola," unpublished Ph.D. diss., Stanford University, 1963 (15th and 16th centuries).

202 ——. "The Performance of Sesquialtera and Hemiola in the 16th Century," JAMS XVII (1964) 5–28.

203 ——. "The Performance of Triplets in the 17th and 18th Centuries," JAMS XIX (1966) 281–328.

204 *The Compleat Musick-Master*, preface by T[homas] B[rown]. London: 1704 (violin).

205 *The Compleat Tutor For the German Flute . . .*, trans. from French. London: Sam Weaver, [ca. 1746] (incl. ornamentation, articulation).

206 *The Compleat Tutor for the Violin. . . .* London: Sam Weaver, [ca. 1746].

207 Cone, Edward T. *Musical Form and Musical Performance*. New York: W. W. Norton, 1968.

208 Conforto, Giovanni Luca. *Brene e facile meniera d'essercitarsi . . . a far passaggi*. Rome: [n. p.], 1593 [?1603]. Fac. and Ger. trans., ed. by J. Wolf. Berlin: Verlag Martin Breslauer, 1922 (vocal ornamentation).

209 ——. *Passaggi sopra tutti li salmi*. Venice: Angelo Gardano fratelli, 1607 (vocal).

209.01 Conrad, F. "Die Verzierung in der Barockmusik. Versuch einer methodisch-praktischen Anleitung für Melodie-instrumenten," *Hausmusik* XX (1956) 157–69.

210 Cooper, Kenneth and Julius Zsako. "Georg Muffat's Observations on the Lully Style of Performance," MQ LIII (1967) 220–45 (incl. tempo, ornaments) (cf. Muffat, Georg, "Florilegium . . .").

211 Corder, Frederick. *Vocal Recitative Historically and Practically Described*. London: Associated Board of the Royal Schools of Music, [ca. 1922] (*secco* vs. *stromentato*, improvisation, rhythm, accompaniment).

212 Corelli, Arcangelo. *Sonate a violino e violone o cimbalo. Opera quinta, parte prima. Troisième édition ou l'on a joint les agrémens . . . composez par Mr. A. Corelli comme il les joue*. Amsterdam: Estienne Roger, [ca. 1715] (ornamentation).

213 Corfe, Joseph. *Thorough Bass Simplified. . . .* London: Printed and published by Preston at his Wholesale Warehouses, [18—], (exx. from Handel, Corelli, Geminiani, Tartini, Sacchini, *et al.*).

213.001 ——. *A Treatise on Singing. . . .* [Salisbury: the author, ca. 1800] (tone production; exx. of Jommelli and Sacchini).

213.002 Corrêa de Araujo, Francisco. *Libro de Tientos y Discvrsos de Mvsica Practica, y Theoricade Organo. . . .* Alcala: Antonio Arnao, 1626 (esp. registration).

213.01 Corrette, Michel. *L'art de se perfectionner dans le violon*. Paris: L'auteur, [1783?].

213.02 ——. *La belle vielleuse*, . . . Paris: chez les Marchands assortis, [ca. 1780] (fingering, tuning, cadences).

214 ——. *L'école d'Orphée: Méthode pour apprendre facilement à jouer du violin*. Paris: 1738.

215 ——. *Le maître de clavecin pour l'accompagnement*. . . . Paris: L'auteur [etc.], 1753.

216 ——. *Méthode pour apprendre aisément à joüer de la flute traversière*. Paris: L'auteur, [177–?].

217 ——. *Méthode, théorique et pratique pour apprendre en peu de tems le violoncelle*. Paris: L'auteur, 1741 (incl. bowing, fingering, ornamentation).

218 ——. *Le parfait maître à chanter* . . ., Nouv. ed. Paris: L'Auteur, [1782].

219 Corri, Domenico. *The Singer's Preceptor* . . ., 2 vols. London: Chappell & Co. [1811]. Ed. by E. Foreman in *The Porpora Tradition*. Champaign: Pro Musica Press, 1968 (cf. Nathan, *Musurgia* . . .) (incl. ornamentation, improvisation).

220 ——. *A Treatise on the Art of Singing*. London: Metzler & Co., [1799] (incl. ornamentation, improvisation).

220.01 Corri, Philip Anthony. "Original System of Preluding," Part IV of *L'anima di Musica*. London: Chappell & Co., [18—] (piano).

221 Cortolegis, Fritz. "Gedanken über eine stilgerechte Aufführung des 'Fidelio,'" Neues Beethoven Jb III (1927) 93–105 (tempo).

222 Costeley, Guillaume. Preface to *Musique de Guillaume Costeley (1570)*, Expert MMRF XVIII (accompaniment).

223 Couperin, François. *L'art de toucher le clavecin*. Paris: L'auteur, 1717. Ed. by A. Linde, with Eng. tr. by M. Roberts. Wiesbaden: Breitkopf & Härtel, [1933].

224 ——. *Œuvres Complètes*, Vol. I; *Œuvres Didactiques*, ed. by M. Cauchie.. Paris: L'Oiseau Lyre, 1933 (incl. "Regle pour L'Acompagnement" and "L'Art de Toucher le Clavecin").

225 ——. Preface to *Pièces de Clavecin (1713)*, *Le Trésor des Pianistes* III (incl. table of ornaments).

226 Courcy, Florence de. *The Art of Singing*. London: [ca. 1868].

226.01 Cowling, Elizabeth. "The Italian Sonata Literature for the Violoncello in the Baroque Era," unpublished Ph.D. diss., Northwestern University, 1967 (incl. *b. c.*, instrumentation).

226.02 Crane, Frederick. *Materials for the Study of the Fifteenth Century Basse Danse*. Brooklyn: The Institute of Mediaeval Music Ltd., 1968 (quotes treatises, dances with steps, incl. bibliography).

227 Crotch, William. *Practical Thorough Bass*. . . . London: Royal Harmonic Institution, [182–?]. (Exx. incl. Luther, Farrant, Cavalieri,

Gibbons, Dowland, Carissimi, A. Scarlatti, Corelli, Handel,
J. S. Bach, Gluck, Haydn).

228 Cucuel, Georges. "Les aventures d'un organiste dauphinois," RM1 I
(1917–19) 106–13 (harpsichord-piano).

229 ——. "La question des clarinettes dans l'instrumentation du XVIIIᵉ
siècle," ZIMG XII (1910–11) 280–84.

229.01 Curtis, Alan Stanley. "Sweelinck's Keyboard Works: A Study of
English Elements in Dutch Secular Music of the *Gouden Eeuw*,"
unpublished Ph.D. diss., University of Illinois, 1963 (ornamentation, chromaticism, temperament).

229.02 Czerny, Carl. *L'art d'improviser* . . . , *Op. 200*. Paris: chez Maurice
Schlesinger, [18—] (some useful material for cadenzas, late
18th century).

230 ——. *Complete Theoretical and Practical Piano Forte School* [*Vollständige
theoretisch-praktische Piano-forte-Schule*, op. 500]. London: [1839].

231 ——. *Letters on Thorough-Bass* . . . , trans. by J. A. Hamilton. London:
R. Cocks and Co., 1896 (incl. expression, articulation).

232 ——. *Über den richtigen Vortrag der sämtlichen Beethovenschen Klavierwerke*
. . . , ed. with commentary by P. Badura-Skoda. Vienna:
Universal Edition, 1963.

D

233 Dadelsen, Georg von. "Verzierungen," MGG XIII Col. 1526–56
(incl. bibliography).

234 Daffner, Hugo. "Was bedeutet 'Basso' in Mozarts Kammermusik?"
Mk VI/1 (1906–07) 297–99 (instrumentation).

235 Dahlhaus, Carl. "Zur Entstehung des modernen Taktsystems im 17.
Jahrhundert," AfMw XVIII (1961) 223–40 (incl. rhythm and
tempo).

236 ——. "Zur Theorie des Tactus im 16. Jahrhundert," AfMw XVII
(1960) 22–39.

237 Dalla Casa, Girolamo. *Il vero modo di diminuir*. 2 vols. Venice: Aug.
Gardano, 1584.

237.01 Danby, J[ohn]. *La Guida alla Musica Vocale*. . . . London: for the
Author, [1787?] (incl. ornaments).

238 Dandrieu, Jean François. *Principes de l'Accompagnement du Clavecin*. . .
Paris: L'auteur, [1718].

239 Danjou, Jean-Louis-Félix. "Lettres d'Italies à Mgr. l'Évêque de
Langres," *Revue de la musique religieuse* III (1847) 129–41
(Roman performance of early music).

240 ——. "Lettres d'Italies à M. Simon," *Revue de la musique religieuse* III
(1847) 161–68 (Roman performance of early music).

241 Dannreuther, Edward. *Musical Ornamentation*, 2 vols. London: Novello
and Co., [1893–95].

241.01 ——. "Notes on the Text of Beethoven," MMR II (1872) 107–70,

33

and III (1873) 2–5, 42–43 (Beethoven's later work, esp. ornamentation, articulation).

242 ——. "Die Verzierungen in den Werken von Johann Sebastian Bach," BJ VI (1909) 41–101 (abridged version of No. 241).

243 Dart, Thurston. "Francesco Geminiani and the Rule of Taste," *The Consort*, no. 19 (July 1962) 122–27 (cf. Geminiani, *Art of Playing on the Violin*).

244 ——. "Handel and the Continuo," MT CVI (1965) 348–50.

244.01 ——. "How They Sang in Jena in 1598," MT CVIII (1967) 316–17.

245 ——. *The Interpretation of Music.* London: Hutchison and Company, 1954 (incl. bibliography).

246 ——. "Miss Mary Burwell's Instruction Book for the Lute," GSJ XI (1958) 3–62 (lute technique, ornaments, tablatures).

247 ——. "Performance Practice in the 17th and 18th Centuries: Six Problems in Instrumental Music," KONGRESS 1961 (New York) 231–35 (incl. keyboard instruments, lute, bowed strings, "flute," harpsichord registration, *notes inégales*).

247.01 ——. "Recorder 'Gracings' in 1700," GSJ XII (1959) 93–94 (quotes British Mus. Add. MS 35043, incl. realizations).

248 Daube, Johann Friedrich. *General-Bass in drey Accorden.* Leipzig: Johann Benjamin Andrae, 1756.

248.01 David, François. *Méthode Nouvelle ou principes generaux pour apprendre facilement la musique, et l'art de chanter.* Paris: Mᵉ La Vᵉ Boivin [etc.], 1737 (incl. ornaments).

249 David, Hans Theodore. *J. S. Bach's Musical Offering: History, Interpretation, and Analysis.* New York: G. Schirmer, 1945 (incl. settings).

250 —— and Arthur Mendel. *The Bach Reader*, rev. ed. New York: W. W. Norton, 1966.

250.001 Davies, Fanny. "About Schumann's Pianoforte Music," MT LI (1910) 493–94 (incl. articulation, dynamics).

250.01 ——. "On Schumann—and Reading Between the Lines," ML VI (1925) 214–23 (esp. piano music).

251 Deas, Stewart. "Beethoven's Allegro assai," ML XXXI (1950) 333–36.

252 Dehn, Siegfried Wilhelm. *Theoretisch-praktische Harmonielehre mit angefügten Generalbass-beispielen.* Berlin: Verlag von Wilhelm Thome, 1840 (18th-century exx., incl. Graun, Corelli, Kirnberger, A. Scarlatti).

253 Deldevez, Edouard-Marie-Ernest. *L'Art du Chef d'Orchestre.* Paris: Firmin-Didot et cⁱᵉ., 1878 (esp. opera).

253.01 ——. "De l'Interprétation des authors classiques," *Curiosités Musicales.* Paris: Librairie de Firmin Didot Frères, Fils et Cie, 1873 181–213 (expression, articulation, tempo, esp. of Haydn, Mozart, Beethoven, Weber).

254 Della Corte, Andrea. *L'Interpretazione musicale e gli interpreti.* [Turin]: Unione tipografico—editrice torinese, [1951].

254.01 Denis, Jean. *Traité de l'accord de l'espinette, avec la comparaison de son Clavier à la Musique vocale.* Paris: Robert Ballard, 1650 (esp. ch. 4).

255 Dennerlein, Hans. "Zum Orgelgebrauch in Mozarts Messen," Mozart Jb (1955) 113–16 (incl. dynamics, registration).

255.01 Devienne, François. *Méthode de Flûte,* new ed. Paris: chez B. Pollet, [n. d.] (articulation, ornamentation).

255.02 ——. *Nouvelle Méthode Théorique et Pratique pour la Flûte.* . . . Paris: chez Imbault, [1800] (esp. ornaments, articulation).

256 Devoto, Daniel. "La Enumeración de instrumentos musicales en la poesia medieval Castellana," Festschrift ANGLÉS 211–22.

256.01 Dieupart, Charles. Preface to *Six Suites de clavecin.* Amsterdam: Estienne Roger, [n. d.]. Ed. by P. Brunold. Paris: Éditions de l'Oiseau Lyre, [ca. 1934] (ornamentation).

256.02 *Directions for Playing on the Flute.* . . . London: Benjamin Cooke, [173–?] (recorder graces, articulation, incl. lexicon)

257 Diruta, Girolamo. *Il Transilvano. Dialogo sopra il vero modo di sonar organi, & istromenti da penna.* Venice: Alessandro Vincenti, 1625 (incl. ornamentation, esp. *tremolo,* and passage-work).

258 Disertori, Benvenuto. "Pratica e tecnica della lira da braccio," RMI XLV (1941) 150–75 (16th and 17th centuries).

259 Distler, Hugo. "Gedanken zum Problem der Registrierung alter, speziell Bachscher Orgelmusik," MuK XI (1939) 101–06.

260 Dodge, Janet. "Ornamentation as indicated by Signs in Lute Tablature," SIMG IX (1907–08) 318–36.

260.01 Dodge, Roger Pryor. "The Importance of Dance Style in the Presentation of Early Western Instrumental Music," MR XVI (1955) 313–22 (esp. Bach keyboard).

260.02 Dodwell, Henry. *A Treatise concerning the Lawfulness of Instrumental Musick in Holy Offices.* London: Henry Clements, 1700 (organ).

261 Döbereiner, Christian. "Über die Viola da Gamba und ihre Verwendung bei Joh. Seb. Bach," BJ VIII (1911) 75–85.

262 ——. *Zur Renaissance alter Musik (Abhandlungen über alte Musikpraxis),* 2nd ed. Tutzing: Hans Schneider, 1960 (incl. ornamentation).

263 Dolmetsch, Arnold. *The Interpretation of the Music of the XVIIth and XVIIIth Centuries Revealed by Contemporary Evidence,* rev. ed. London; Novello, 1946 (esp. articulation).

263.01 Dolmetsch, Carl. "Interpretation," *The Consort* No. 5 (1948) 7–12.

263.02 ——. "Observations on the Legitimate Use of Alternative Instruments in Early Music," *The Consort* No. 10 (1953) 17–20.

263.03 Dolmetsch, Cecile. "Ornamentation in Singing," *The Consort* No. 9 (1952) 21–23.

264 Doni, Giovanni Battista. "Trattato della musica scenica [ca. 1635],"

Trattati di musica, ed. by A. F. Gori, II. Florence: 1763 1–144 and Appendix.

265 Donington, Robert. *The Interpretation of Early Music*, 2nd ed. New York: St. Martin's Press, 1965 (incl. bibliography).

266 ——. "On Interpreting Early Music," ML XXVIII (1947) 223–41 (ornaments, bowing).

267 ——. "Performing Purcell's Music Today," *Henry Purcell (1659–1695)*: *Essays on his Music*, ed. by I. Holst. London: Oxford University Press, 1959 74–102 (incl. *b. c.*, vocal embellishment, *notes inégales*).

268 ——. "A Problem of Inequality," MQ LIII (1967) 503–17 (*notes inégales*).

269 ——. *Tempo and Rhythm in Bach's Organ Music.* London: Henrichsen Edition, 1960.

269.01 Donington, Robert & George J. Buelow. "Figured Bass as Improvisation," AMl XL (1968) 178–79 (cf. Oberdörffer, "Neuere Generalbassstudien.").

270 Dorian, Frederick. *The History of Music in Performance.* . . . New York: W. W. Norton, 1942.

271 Douglass, Fenner and M. A. Verte. "French Organ Registration in the Early 16th Century," MQ LI (1965) 614–35.

271.001 Dounias, M. *Die Violinkonzerte Giuseppe Tartinis als Ausdruck einer Künstlerpersönlichkeit und einer Kulturepoche.* Wolfenbüttel & Berlin: Georg Kallmeyer-Verlag, 1935 170–85 (ornamentation).

271.002 Dowland, Robert. *Varietie of Lute-lessons.* . . . London: Thomas Adams, 1610. Fac. ed. by E. Hunt. London: Schott & Co., 1958 (esp. tuning, right-hand technique).

271.01 Downes, Edward O. D. "*Secco* Recitative in Early Classical Opera Seria (1720–80)," JAMS XIV (1961) 50–69.

271.02 Downes, Ralph. "Interpretation of Classic Organ Music," *The Consort* No. 5 (1948) 17–21 (incl. ornamentation).

272 Drechsler, Joseph. *Harmonie und Generalbass-Lehre.* Vienna: S. A. Steiner and Co., [181–] (Library of Congress copy has 1st 27 pp. in handwritten translation into Eng. by E. Hodges).

273 Drinker, Henry S. *Bach's Use of Slurs in Recitativo Secco.* Princeton: Association of American Choruses, 1946.

274 Duckles, Vincent. "Florid Embellishment in English Song of the Late 16th and Early 17th Centuries," AnnMl V (1957) 329–45.

275 Dürr, Alfred. "Zum Problem 'Concertisten' und 'Ripienisten' in der H-Moll Messe," MuK XXXI (1961) 232–36 (cf. Ehmann, "'Concertisten' und 'Ripienisten' . . .").

276 ——. "Zur Aufführungspraxis der Vor-Leipziger Kirchenkantaten J. S. Bachs," MuK XX (1950) 54–64.

276.01 Dürr, Walther. "Formen und Möglichkeiten des musikalischen

Vortrages," Mf XXI (1968) 182–98 (declamation, 17th to 20th centuries).

277 ——. Studien zu Rhythmus und Metrum im italienischen Madrigal, insbesondere bei Luca Marenzio," unpublished Ph.D. diss., Tübingen, 1956.

278 ——. "Zum Verhältnis von Wort und Ton im Rhythmus des Cinquecento-Madrigals," Af Mf XV (1958) 89–100.

279 Dufourcq, Norbert. "Concerts parisiens et Associations de 'Symphonistes' . . ., RB VIII (1954) 46–55 (incl. works performed).

279.01 Duncan, Edmondstoune. "Of the Lute or Theorbo," MMR XXXII (1902) 65 (17th-century instrumentation).

279.02 Dunn, John Petrie. *Ornamentation in the Works of Frederick Chopin.* London: Novello, [1921].

279.03 Dupuit, Jean Baptiste. *Principes pour toucher de la vielle avec six sonates pour cet instrument qui conviennent aux Violon, flûte, clavessin. . . .* Oeuvre I. Paris: l'Auteur, [1741].

280 Durante, Ottavio. *Arie devote le quali contengono in sè la maniera de cantar con grazio l'imitazione delle parole e il modo di scriver passaggi ed altri affetti.* Rome: Simone Verovio, 1608.

280.001 Durieu. . . . *Nouvelle méthode de musique vocale. . . .* Paris: l'Auteur, [1793] (incl. ornaments).

E

280.002 Ebers, Karl Friedrich. *Vollständige Singschule.* Mainz: bei B. Schott, [17—] (comprehensive, incl. ornaments, dynamics, recitative, tempo, articulation, phrasing, cadences).

280.01 Egan, Patricia. "'Concert' Scenes in Musical Paintings of the Italian Renaissance," JAMS XIV (1961) 184–95 (negative iconography).

281 Ehmann, Wilhelm. "Aufführungspraxis der Bachschen Motteten," MuK XXI (1951) 49–67. Also in *Kongress-Bericht, Gesellschaft für Musikforschung Lüneburg 1950*, ed. by H. Albrecht, H. Osthoff and W. Wiora. Kassel: Bärenreiter-Verlag, 1950 121–123.

282 ——. "'Concertisten' und 'Ripienisten' in der H-Moll Messe Joh. Seb. Bachs," MuK XXX (1960) 95–104, 138–47, 227–36, 255–73, 298–309 (cf. Dürr, "'Concertisten' . . .").

283 ——. "Heinrich Schütz: Die Psalmen Davids, 1619, in der Aufführungspraxis," MuK XXVI (1956) 145–71 (setting, *b. c.*).

284 ——. "Klaviermusik und Klavierinstrument bei J. S. Bach," *Das Musikleben* VI (1953) 43–46 (clavichord-harpsichord).

285 ——. "Noch einmal zum Problem: 'Concertisten-Ripienisten,'" MuK XXXI (1961) 267–71 (cf. *supra*).

286 ——. "'Was guett auff Posaunen ist, etc.'" ZfMw XVII (1935) 171–75 (instrumentation in 16th-century sacred music).

286.01 Ehrlich, Heinrich. *The Ornamentation in Beethoven's Pianoforte-Works,* Eng. trans. by H. Brett. Leipzig: Steingräber Verlag, 1896 (incl. tempo, accidentals).

286.02 ———. *The Ornaments in Johann Sebastian Bach's Pianoforte-Works,* Eng. trans. by H. Brett. Leipzig: Steingräber-Edition, [1898].

287 Eibner, Franz. "The Dotted-Quaver-and-Semiquaver Figure with Triplet Accompaniment in the Works of Schubert," trans. by M. J. E. Brown, MR XXIII (1962) 281–84.

287.01 Eichborn, Hermann. "Die Clarintrompeterei," MWb XVI (1885) 622–24, 638–39 (Baroque).

288 Einstein, Alfred. "Il conflitto fra la parola e il suono," RaM XXV (1955) 1–16 (rondeaux, laude, *etc.*, 12th–14th centuries).

288.01 ———. *Zur deutschen Literatur für Viola da gamba im 16. und 17. Jahrhundert.* [Leipzig: Breitkopf & Härtel, 1905] (ornamentation).

289 [Eitner, Robert]. "Eine Musiklehre des 17. Jahrhunderts," MfM XI (1879) 17–27 (description of keyboard fingering, accompaniment; also quotes Carissimi's *Ars Cantandi* on vocal ornamentation).

290 ———. "Einiges aus Michael Praetorius Syntagma musicum, 3. Tomus, Wolfenbüttel 1619," MfM X (1878) 33–44, 49–54 (instrumentation, conducting, ornaments, dynamics).

291 ———. "Heinrich Albert über das Generalbass-Spiel," MfM XV (1883) 70–73 (Preface to *Günstigen Music-Freund,* 1651).

292 [———]. "Hermann Finck über die Kunst des Singens, 1556," MfM XI (1879) 129–33, 135–41, 151–66 (*Practica Musica V,* vocal ornamentation).

293 [———]. "Johannes de Grocheo's Lehren über die weltliche Musik des Mittlelalters," trans. by J. Wolf, MfM XXXIII (1901) 41–47 (Ars Antiqua, setting).

294 ———. "Quantz und Emanuel Bach," MfM XXXIV (1902) 39–46, 55–63 (ornamentation, *b. c.,* tempo).

295 Ellinwood, Leonard (ed.). Introduction to *The Works of Francesco Landini.* Cambridge: The Mediaeval Academy of America, 1939 (instrumentation).

295.01 Elsen, Josephine Caryce. "The Instrumental Works of Peter Ritter," unpublished Ph.D. diss., Northwestern University, 1967 (incl. rhythm, instrumentation).

296 Elsner, Emilie. "Untersuchung der instrumentalen Besetzungspraxis der weltlichen Musik im 16. Jahrhundert in Italien," Ohlau i. Schl.: Dr. H. Escherhagen, KG, [1935] (strings vs. winds).

297 Elston, Arnold. "On Musical Dynamics," unpublished Ph.D. diss., Harvard University, 1939.

298 Elvers, Rudolf. "Untersuchungen zu den Tempi in Mozarts Instrumentalmusik," unpublished Ph.D. diss., Berlin, 1952.

298.01 Emery, Walter. "Bach's Keyboard Partitas: A Set of Composer's Corrections?" MT XCIII (1952) 495–99.

299 ———. *Bach's Ornaments.* London: Novello, 1953.

299.01 ———. "Bach's Ornaments," MT LXXXIX (1948) 43–45.

300 ———. "The Interpretation of Bach. A Note on Additional Ornaments and Rhythmic Alteration," MT XCVI (1955) 190–93.

300.01 ———. "New Methods in Bach Editing," MT XCI (1950) 297–99 (deals with variants between MSS).

300.02 ———. "On the Registration of Bach's Organ Preludes and Fugues," MT CIII (1962) 396–98, 467–69.

301 Enderle, Hermann. "Binäre gegen ternäre Rhythmen bei J. S. Bach— Notation und Ausführung," MuK XXXVI (1966) 17–18 (*notes inégales*).

301.01 ———. "Nochmals zum Thema 'Binäre gegen ternäre Rhythmen bei J. S. Bach,'" Muk XXXVII (1967) 69–73.

302 Engel, Hans. "Diminution," MGG III Col. 489–504 (incl. bibliography).

303 ———. "Mozarts Instrumentation," Mozart Jb (1956) 51–74.

304 ———. "Nochmals die Intermedien von Florenz 1589," Festschrift SCHNEIDER (80) 71–86 (incl. instrumentation).

305 ———. "Probleme der Aufführungspraxis," Mozart Jb (1955) 56–65 (incl. instrumentation, ornamentation, dynamics).

306 Engelke, Hans. "A Study of Ornaments in American Tune Books, 1760–1800," unpublished Ph.D. diss., University of Southern California, 1960.

307 Engländer, Richard. "Aufführungsstil," *Joseph Martin Kraus und die Gustavianische Oper.* Leipzig: Harrassowitz, 1943 31–42 (ensembles and facilities).

307.01 Epstein, Lonny. "Thoughts on Phrasing in Mozart's Piano Works," *Juilliard Review* III/2 (1956) 27–32.

308 Eras, Rudolf. "Über das Verhältnis zwischen Stimmung und Spieltechnik bei Streichinstrumenten in Da-gamba-Haltung," unpublished Ph.D. diss., Leipzig, 1958.

309 Ernst, Friedrich. "Bach und das Pianoforte," BJ XLVIII (1961) 61–78.

310 Evans, Kenneth Gene. "Instructional Materials for the Oboe, 1695– *ca.* 1800," unpublished Ph.D. diss., State University of Iowa, 1963 (incl. terms, symbols, rhythm, ornaments, tone production, articulation).

311 Evenson, Pattee Edward. "A History of Brass Instruments, Their Usage, Music, and Performance Practices in Ensembles During the Baroque Era," unpublished Ph.D. diss., University of Southern California, 1960.

311.01 Falck, Georg. . . . *Idea boni cantoris.* . . . Nuremberg: gedruckt bey W. M. Endter, 1688 (esp. diminutions).

312 Falkener, Robert. *Instructions for Playing the Harpsichord.* . ., 2nd ed. London: Printed and sold by the author, 1774 (incl. *b. c.*, tuning).

313 Faller, Hedwig. *Die Gesangskoloratur in Rossinis Opern und ihre Ausfuhrung.* Berlin: Triltsch & Huther, 1935.

314 Fano, Fabio (ed.). "La Camerata Fiorentina, Vincenzo Galilei (1520? –1591). . ." *Istituzioni e monumenti dell'arte musicale italiana* IV. Milan: Ricordi, 1934 (reproduces Galilei's "Dialogo della Musica . . ." and related prefaces).

315 Farmer, Henry George. "The Great Kettledrums of the Royal Artillery," *Handel's Kettledrums and Other Papers on Military Music.* London: Hinrichsen, 1965, 85–96.

316 Fasano, Renato. *Storia degli abbellimenti musicali.* Rome: De Santis, 1947.

316.01 Faure, J. *La Voix et le Chant.* Paris: Henri Heugel, [n. d.] (technique, ornaments).

317 Faustini-Fasini, Eugenia. "Gli astri maggiori del 'bel canto' Napoletano," *Note d'Archivio* XII (1935) 297–316; XV (1938) 121–28, 157–70 (18th century, chronological).

317.01 Fay, Harry F. *Ornaments in Music.* Boston: Miles & Thompson, 1893 (keyboard).

318 Feil, Arnold. "Zur Rhythmik Schuberts," KONGRESS 1962 (Kassel) 198–200.

319 Fekete, Zoltan. "Händel und die Aufführungspraxis," Österr MZ II (1947) 286–88 (orchestration).

320 Fellerer, Karl Gustav. "Das Partimentospiel, eine Aufgabe des Organisten im 18. Jahrhundert," KONGRESS 1930 (Liège) 109–12 (*b. c.*).

321 Fellinger, Imogen. *Studien zur Dynamik in Brahms' Musik.* Berlin: Hesses Verlag, 1961.

322 ——. "Zum Problem der Zeitmasse in Brahms' Musik," KONGRESS 1962 (Kassel) 219–22.

323 Fellowes, Edmund Horace (ed.). *The English School of Lutenist Song Writers*, Series 2, Vol. I. London: Stainer & Bell, 1925 (Campian's "To the Reader" incl. doubling).

324 Fenaroli, Fedele. *Metodo nuovamente riformato de' partimenti.* Milan: G. Ricordi, [18—].

325 ——. *Regole musicali per i principianti di cembalo.* . . . Naples: [n. p.], 1775 (*b. c.*).

326 Ferand, Ernest T. "Embellished 'Parody Cantatas' in the Early 18th Century," MQ XLIV (1958) 40–64 (incl. *b. c.*).

327 ——. "Guillaume Guerson's Rules of Improvised Counterpoint (c. 1500)," Festschrift ANGLÉS 253–63.

328 ——. *Die Improvisation in Beispielen aus neun Jahrhunderten abendländischer Musik.* Cologne: Arno Volk Verlag, [ca. 1956]. Eng. ed. as *Improvisation in Nine Centuries of Western Music.* . . . Cologne: Arno Volk Verlag [c. 1961].

329 ——. "Improvised Vocal Counterpoint in the Late Renaissance and Early Baroque," AnnM1 IV (1956) 129–74.

330 ——. "Improvvisazioni e composizioni polifoniche," RMI LIV (1952) 128–38.

331 Ferguson, Howard. "Bach's 'Lauten Werck,'" ML XLVIII (1967) 259–64.

332 —— (ed.). Prefaces to *Style and Interpretation: An Anthology of 16th–19th Century Keyboard Music,* 4 vols. London: Oxford University Press, 1963.

333 ——. "Repeats and Final Bars in the Fitzwilliam Virginal Book," ML XLIII (1962) 345–50.

334 Finck, Hermann. *Practica Musica Hermanni Finckii.* . . . Wittenberg: Excusa Typis Haeredum Georgii Rhavv, 1556.

335 Finscher, Ludwig. "Aufführungspraktische Versuche zur geistlichen Musik des 15. und 16. Jahrhunderts im Westdeutschen Rundfunk Köln," Mf XII (1959) 480–88.

336 ——. "Che farò senza Euridice? Ein Beitrag zur Gluck-Interpretation," *Festschrift Hans Engel zum siebzigsten Geburtstag,* ed. H. Heussner. Kassel: Bärenreiter, 1964 96–110.

337 Fiocco, Joseph-Hector. Preface to *Werken voor Clavecimbel,* MMB III (incl. ornaments).

338 Fischer, Johan Philip Albrecht. *Korte en noodigste grond-Regelen van de Bassus-Continuus.* . . . Utrecht: W. Stouw, 1731.

339 Fischer, Kurt von. "Eine Neubearbeitung von L. Mozarts Violinschule aus dem Jahre 1804; Ein Stilvergleich," Mf II (1949) 187–92.

340 Fischer, Martin. *Die organistische Improvisation im 17. Jahrhundert.* Kassel: Bärenreiter, 1929.

341 Fischer, Wilhelm. "Selbstzeugnisse Mozarts für die Aufführungsweise seiner Werke," Mozart Jb (1955) 7–16.

342 ——. "Die sogenannte 'Werktreue,'" Festschrift PAUMGARTNER 12–21.

343 Flade, Ernst. "Literarische Zeugnisse zur Empfindung der *Farbe* und *Farbigkeit* bei der Orgel und beim Orgelspiel in Deutschland ca. 1500–1620," AM1 XXVIII (1956) 176–206.

344 Flögel, Bruno. "Studien zur Arientechnik in den Opern Händels," Händel Jb (1929) 50–156.

344.01 *The Flute-Master Compleat Improv'd.* . . . London: John Young, 1706 (fingering, articulation, graces).

345 Förster, Emmanuel Aloys. *Anleitung zum General-Bass.* Vienna: Artaria Comp., [1805].

346 Foesel, Karl. "Untersuchungen zur Spielmethodik der Hammerklaviere," unpublished Ph.D. diss., Erlangen, 1942.

346.001 Forbes, Watson. "On Performing Bach's 'Musical Offering,'" MT LXXXIX (1948) 330–35, 365–67.

346.01 Forte, John F. "Mozart's Pianoforte Works" ML VII (1926) 374–77.

346.02 Fortune, Nigel. "Italian 17th-Century Singing," ML XXXV (1954) 206–19.

347 Fourné, Ferdinand. "Studien zur Entwicklung des Echoprinzips in der Instrumentalmusik des Barocks bis Corelli," unpublished Ph.D. diss., Vienna, 1941.

348 Fowles, Ernest. *Studies in Musical Graces.* Boston: The Boston Music Company, 1907.

348.01 Fox Strangways, Arthur Henry. "Phrasing," ML IX (1928) 1–8 (incl. Bach, Handel, Beethoven, Schumann, Gounod).

349 Frei, Walter. "Die bayerische Hofkapelle unter Orlando di Lasso; Ergänzungen und Berichtigungen zur Deutung von Mielichs Bild," Mf XV (1962) 359–64 (iconography).

350 ———. "Zwei wenig beachtete Grundsätze bei Verwendung von Instrumenten in mittelalterlicher Musik," Mf XVIII (1965) 277–81 (timbre, instrumentation).

350.01 [Freillon Poncein, Jean Pierre]. *La veritable manière d'apprendre à jouer en perfection du hautbois, de la flûte et du flageolet, avec les principes de la musique pour la voix et pour toutes sortes d'instrumens.* Paris: chez Jacques Collombat, 1700.

351 Frescobaldi, Girolamo. Preface to *Toccate.* Rome: P. Masotti, 1628. Reprinted in *Frescobaldi Gesamtausgabe*, Vol. III, ed. P. Pidoux, Kassel: Bärenreiter, 1948.

352 Frey, Martin. "Die Taktart im ersten Satze von Beethovens C-Moll Symphonie," Mk IX/3 (1909–10) 64–70.

353 Frick, Philipp Joseph. *A Treatise on Thorough Bass. . . .* London: Printed for and sold by the author, [1786].

354 Friedemann, Lilli. "Bachspiel für Streicher," *Hausmusik* XIV (1950) 59–62, 114–23.

355 Frotscher, Gotthold. *Aufführungspraxis alter Musik.* Locarno: Heinrichshofen's Verlag, 1963.

355.01 ———. "Zur Registrierkunst des achtzehnten Jahrhunderts," *Bericht über die Freiburger Tagung für deutsche Orgelkunst vom 27. bis 30. Juli 1926*, ed. by W. Gurlitt. Augsburg: Bärenreiter, 1926 70–75 (based on Gronau [Daniel M.]).

355.02 Fruchtman, Efrim and Caroline. "Instrumental Scoring in the Chamber Cantatas of Francesco Conti," Festschrift HAYDON 245–59.

356 Fuller-Maitland, John Alexander. "The Interpretation of Musical Ornaments," KONGRESS 1911 (London) 259–67.

356.01 ——. "The Interpretation of Musical Ornaments," MT LII (1911) 647–51.

357 ——. "A Note on the Interpretation of Musical Ornaments," SIMG XIII (1911–12) 543–51.

358 —— and W. Barclay Squire (eds.). Preface to *The Fitzwilliam Virginal Book*. Leipzig: Breitkopf & Härtel, 1899 (incl. rhythm, ornaments, technique).

G

358.01 Gabriel, Wolfgang. "Dirigent und Barocke Orchestermusik," Österr MZ XXII (1967) 711–21 (incl. instrumentation and tempo).

358.02 Gábry, Gy. "Das Klavier Beethovens und Liszts," SMl VIII (1966) 379–90.

359 Galkin, Elliott Washington. "The Theory and Practice of Orchestral Conducting since 1752," unpublished Ph.D. diss., Cornell University, 1960.

360 Gallo, F. Alberto. "Il 'Saggio per ben sonare il flautotraverso' di Antonio Lorenzoni nella cultura musicale italiana del Settecento," RaM XXXI (1961) 102–11 (discusses Lorenzoni's treatise, 1779).

361 Galpin, the Rev. Francis W. *Old English Instruments of Music: Their History and Character*, 4th ed., rev. by T. Dart. London: Methuen, 1965.

362 Ganassi, Silvestro. *Opera Intitulata Fontegara*. Venice: [n. p.], 1535. Modern ed. by H. Peter. Berlin: Robert Lienau, 1956 (recorder, ornamentation).

363 ——. *Regola Rubertina*. . . . Venice: [n. p.], 1542–43. Fac. ed. by M. Schneider. Leipzig: Fr. Kistner & C. F. W. Siegel, 1924 (viola da gamba).

364 Garcia, Manuel. *Traité complet de l'art du chant*. Paris: 1847. Eng. ed. as *New Treatise on the Art of Singing* . . . , rev. ed. Boston: Oliver Ditson, [187–?].

364.01 Garnsey, Sylvia. "The Use of Hand-plucked Instruments in the Continuo Body: Nicola Matteis," ML XLVII (1966) 135–40 (17th century).

365 Garros, Madeleine. "L'art d'accompagner sur la basse-continue d'après Guillaume-Gabriel Nivers," *Mélanges d'histoire et d'esthétique musicales offerts à Paul-Marie Masson* . . . , II. Paris: Masse, 1955 45–51.

366 Gasparini, Francesco. *L'Armonico pratico al cimbalo*. . . . Venice: Antonio Bortoli, 1708. Trans. by F. S. Stillings as *The Practical Harmonist at the Harpsichord*, and ed. by D. L. Burrows. New Haven: Yale School of Music, 1963.

367 Gassner, Ferdinand Simon. *Dirigent und Ripienist*. . . . Karlsruhe: C. T. Groos, 1844.

367.01 Gatty, Reginald. "Tempo Rubato," MT LIII (1912) 160–62.

368 Gaultier, Denis. Preface to *La Rhétorique des Dieux*, PSFM, Ser. 1, Vol. VI (incl. ornaments).

368.01 Geck, Martin. *Die Wiederentdeckung der Matthäuspassion im 19. Jahrhundert*. Regensburg: Gustav Bosse Verlag, 1967 (incl. bowing, tempo, dynamics, text alterations, esp. 34–60, "Die Aufführung und ihre Aufnahme in der Öffentlichkeit").

368.02 Geer, E. Harold. "Media of Performance," Part IV, *Organ Registration in Theory and Practice*. Glen Rock: J. Fischer & Bros., 1957 225–331 (esp. ch. 10–12).

369 Geminiani, Francesco. *The Art of Accompaniament*. . . . London: for the Author by John Johnson, 1753 (*b. c.*).

370 ——. *The Art of Playing on the Violin . . . Opera IX*. London: [n. p.], 1751. Fac. ed. by D. Boyden. London: Oxford, [1952] (incl. ornamentation, articulation, dynamics).

370.01 ——. *Compleat Instruction for the Violin*. London: G. Goulding, [17—?] (incl. ornamentation).

371 ——. *Rules for playing in a true Taste on the Violin, German Flute, Violoncello and Harpsichord, particularly the Thorough Bass . . . Opera VIII*. London: with His Majesty's Royal Licence, [1745?] (expression).

372 ——. *A Treatise of Good Taste in the Art of Musick*. London: [n. p.], 1749 (incl. ornamentation, dynamics, articulation).

373 Gennrich, Friedrich. "Zur Musikinstrumentenkunde der Machaut-Zeit," ZfMw IX (1926–27) 513–17.

374 Geoffrey-Dechaume, Antoine. *Les "Secrets" de la musique ancienne; recherches sur l'interpretation XVIe–XVIIe–XVIIIe siècles*. Paris: Fasquelle Éditeurs, 1964.

375 Georgii, Walter. *Die Verzierungen in der Musik. Theorie und Praxis*. Zürich: Atlantis Verlag, 1957.

376 Gerhartz, Karl. "Die Violinschule in ihrer musikgeschichtlichen Entwicklung bis Leopold Mozart," ZfMw VII (1924–25) 553–69.

377 ——. "Die Violinschule von Leopold Mozart (1756)," Mozart Jb III (1929) 243–302.

378 ——. "Zur älteren Violintechnik," ZfMw VII (1924–25) 6–12 (Baroque).

378.01 Germer, Heinrich. *Die musikalische Ornamentik*. Leipzig: C. F. Leede, 1878 [NYPL date]. Eng. trans. as *The Technics of Piano-forte-playing. Musical Ornamentation Manual*. Leipzig: C. F. Leede, [ca. 1886].

379 Gérold, Théodore. *L'Art du chant en France au XVIIe siècle*. Strasbourg: Commission des publications de la Faculté des Lettres, 1921 (incl. recitative, ornamentation, pronunciation, articulation).

380 Gerstenberg, Walter. "Andante," KONGRESS 1962 (Kassel) 156–58 (Baroque).

381 ——. "Authentische Tempi für Mozarts 'Don Giovanni?'" Mozart Jb (1960–61) 58–61.

382 ——. "Generalbasslehre und Kompositionstechnik in Niedts 'Musikalischer Handleitung,'" KONGRESS 1953 (Bamberg) 152–55.

383 Ghisi, Federico. "An Angel Concert in a Trecento Sienese Fresco," Festschrift REESE 308–13 (instrumental accompaniment, iconography).

383.01 ——. "Ballet Entertainments in Pitti Palace, Florence, 1608–1625," MQ XXXV (1949) 421–36 (incl. instrumentation).

383.02 ——. "Le musiche per 'Il Ballo di Donne Turche' di Marco da Gagliano," *Revista Italiana di Musicologia* I (1966) 20–30 (early 17th-century instrumentation).

384 ——. "L'Orchestra in Monteverdi," Festschrift FELLERER 187–92.

384.01 Giebler, Albert C. (ed.). Preface to Johann Caspar Kerll's *Missa Superba*. New Haven: A–R Editions, 1967 (solo-tutti, dynamics, accompaniment, tempo).

385 Giegling, Franz. "Der Begriff 'Konzert' in der Barockmusik," SMZ LXXXIV (1944) 381–88 (instrumentation).

386 Gil-Marchex, Henri. "À propos de la technique de piano de Liszt," RM (June, 1928) 76–88.

387 Gindele, Corbinian. "Doppelchor und Psalmvortrag im Frühmittelalter," Mf VI (1953) 296–300.

388 [Giustiniani, Vicenzo]. *Discorso sopra la musica (ca.* 1628), trans. by C. MacClintock. [Rome]: American Institute of Musicology, 1962 (Bound with Bottrigari, *Il Desiderio*) (vocal and instrumental).

389 Goehr, Walter (ed.). Preface to Claudio Monteverdi's *Vespro della Beata Vergine*. Vienna: Universal Edition, 1956 (incl. boys' choir, *falso bordone*, instrumentation).

389.01 Göllner, Theodor. "Eine Spielanweisung für Tasteninstrumente aus dem 15. Jahrhundert," *Essays in Musicology: A Birthday Offering for Willi Apel*, ed. by H. Tischler. Bloomington: School of Music, Indiana University, (1968) 69–81 (incl. tactus, keyboard doubling).

390 Goerges, Horst. *Das Klangsymbol des Todes im dramatischen Werk Mozarts. Studien über ein klangsymbolisches Problem und seine musikalische Gestaltung durch Bach, Händel, Gluck und Mozart.* Wolfenbüttel: Kallmeyer, 1937.

391 Göthel, Folker. *Das Violinspiel Ludwig Spohrs. Unter Berücksichtigung geigentechnischer Probleme seiner Zeit.* Grosschönau i. Sa.: H. Engelhardt, [1935].

392 ——. "Zur Praxis der älteren Violinspiels," *Festschrift Arnold Schering zum sechzigsten Geburtstag, in Verbindung mit Max Schneider und*

45

Gotthold Frotscher, ed. by H. Osthoff, W. Seranky, A. Adrio. Berlin: A. Glas, 1937 96–105.

393 Goldhammer, Otto. "Die neue Liszt-Ausgabe," BzMw II (1960) 69–85 (interpretation).

394 Goldsbrough, Arnold. "Zur Händelschen Aufführungspraxis," Händel Jb (1956) 62–67 (incl. meter, tempo).

395 Goldschmidt, Hugo. "Das Cembalo im Orchester der italienischen Oper zur zweiten Hälfte des 18. Jahrhunderts," *Festschrift zum 90. Geburtstage Sr. Exz. des Wirklichen geheimen Rates Rochus Freiherrn von Liliencron überreicht von Vertretern deutscher Musikwissenschaft.* Leipzig: Breitkopf & Härtel, 1910 87–92.

396 ——. "Die Instrumentalbegleitung der italienischen Musikdramen in der ersten Hälfte des XVII. Jahrhunderts," MfM XXVII (1895) 52–62.

397 ——. *Die italienische Gesangsmethode des XVII. Jahrhunderts.* Breslau: Schlesische Buchdrückerei, Kunst- und verlags-anstalt, vormals S. Schottlaender, 1890.

398 ——. *Die Lehre von der vokalen Ornamentik,* Bd. 1. Charlottenburg: Verlag von Paul Lehsten, 1907.

399 ——. "Das Orchester der italienischen Oper im 17. Jahrhundert," SIMG II (1900–1901) 16–75.

400 ——. "Verzierungen, Veränderungen und Passaggien im 16. und 17. Jahrhundert, und ihre musikalische Bedeutung besprochen nach zwei bisher unbekannten Quellen," MfM XXIII (1891) 111–126 (vocal ornamentation according to Bacilly's *L'Art du bien chanter* and Bovicelli's *Regole . . .*).

401 ——. "Zur Frage der vokalen Auszierung Händel'scher Oratorien," AMz XXXV (1908) 380.

401.001 Goldthwaite, Scott. "Ornamentation in Music for the Keyboard," (Summy Piano Teaching Pamphlet Ser. 5) Chicago: C. F. Summy Co., [195–] (mainly 17th–18th centuries).

401.01 Gombosi, Otto. "About Dance and Dance Music in the Late Middle Ages," MQ XXVII (1941) 289–305 (incl. instrumentation).

402 ——. "About Organ Playing in the Divine Service, circa 1500," Festschrift DAVISON 51–68 (alteration practice).

403 —— (ed.). Preface to Thomas Stoltzer's *Psalm 86,* "Herr, neige deine Ohren." St. Louis: Concordia, 1953 (accentuation).

404 Gottlieb, Robert. "Französischer, italienischer und vermischter Stil in den Solosonaten Georg Friedrich Händels," Händel Jb (1966) 93–108 (incl. ornamentation, rhythm, tempo).

404.01 Goudar, Ange. *Le Brigandage de la Musique Italienne.* Amsterdam: [n. p.], 1780 (Italian opera).

405 Graaf, Christiaan Ernst. *Proeve over de natuur der harmonie in de generaal bas. . . .* 's Gravenhage: B. Wittelaer, 1782.

405.01 Greeting, Thomas. *The Pleasant Companion: or New Lessons and*

Instructions for the Flagelet. 2nd ed. London: J. Playford, 1673 (fingering, articulation).

405.02 Grétry, André Ernest Modeste. *Méthode simple pour apprendre à pré luder.* . . . Paris: de l'imprimerie de la République, [1802].

405.03 Greulich, Martin. *Beiträge zur Geschichte des Streichinstrumentenspiels im 16. Jahrhundert.* Saalfeld: Günthers Buchdruckerei, [1933] (viol, lira).

405.04 Griepenkerl, F. K. "Metronomic Marks for J. S. Bach's Organ Works," MMR VI (1876) 185.

406 Griffi, Horatio (ed.). Preface to Giovanni Francesco Anerio's *Teatro Armonico Spirituale di Madrigali (1619).* VogelB I 18 (early oratorio and immediate antecedents).

406.001 Grimarest, Jean Leonar le Gallois de. *Traité du récitatif.* . . . Paris: Jaques le Fevre et Pierre Ribou, 1707 (incl. accents, pronunciation).

406.01 Grundmann, Herbert. "Per il Clavicembalo o Piano-Forte," Festschrift SCHMIDT-GÖRG (70) 100–17 (Haydn).

407 Grunsky, Karl. "Ein Blick ins Wagnersche Orchester," Mk XXV (1933) 731–36.

408 Gugl, Matthaeus. *Fundamenta partiturae in compendio data.* . . . Augsburg: Joseph Wolf, 1777 (*b. c.*).

409 Gugler, Bernhard. "Vorübergehender Taktwechsel bei Händel," AmZ, Ser. 3, Vol. X (1875) 177–82.

410 Gui, Vittorio. "La Funzione dell' esecutore," Festschrift MARINUZZI 47–68.

411 Gullo, Salvatore. *Das Tempo in der Musik des XIII. und XIV. Jahrhunderts.* Bern: Paul Haupt, 1964.

411.01 Gunn, John. *The Art of Playing the German-Flute on new principles.* . . . London: by the author, [1793] (tone, fingering, articulation ornaments, expression).

H

412 Haas, Robert M. *Aufführungspraxis der Musik.* Wildpark-Potsdam: Akademische Verlagsgesellschaft Athenaion, 1931 (incl. bibliography).

413 ———. "Zur Frage der Orchester besetzungen in der 2. Hälfte des 18. Jahrhunderts," *Bericht . . . III. Kongress der Internationalen Musikgesellschaft Wien* 25. bis 29. Mai, 1909. Vienna: Artaria & Co., 1909 159–67 (make-up of various orchestras).

413.01 Habeneck, François Antoine. *Méthode Théorique et Pratique de Violon.* Paris: chez Canaux, [ca. 1835] (based on MS notes by Viotti).

414 Haböck, Franz. *Die Kastraten und ihre Gesangskunst.* Berlin and Leipzig: Deutsche Verlags-Anstalt Stuttgart, 1927.

415 Häfner, Roland. *Die Entwicklung der Spieltechnik und der Schul- und Lehrwerke für Klavierinstrumente.* Munich: Musikwissenschaftliches Seminar der Universität, 1937.

416 Hahn, Georg Joachim Joseph. *Der nach der neuern Art wohl unterwiesene General-Bass-Schüler . . .,* 2nd ed. Augsburg: Johann Jacob Lotter, 1768.

417 ——. *Der wohl unterwiesene General-Bass-Schüler.* Augsburg: J. J. Lotters seel. Erben, 1751.

418 Halfpenny, Eric. "Bow (1)," *Grove D.,* 5th ed., I 853–54.

419 ——. "The French Hautboy: A Technical Survey," GSJ VI (1953) 23–34, VIII (1955) 50–59 (discusses embouchure, hand positions, reed, intonation).

420 ——. "Sound Hole," *Grove D.,* 5th ed., VII 1001–03.

421 Hall, James S. and Martin V. Hall. "Handel's Graces," Händel Jb (1957) 25–43.

422 Hamburger, Povl. "The Ornamentations in the Works of Palestrina," AM1 XXII (1950) 128–47.

422.01 Hamilton, Clarence G. *Ornaments in Classical and Modern Music.* Boston: Oliver Ditson Co., 1930 (incl. tempo).

423 Hammerschlag, János. "Sigel-Ornamente in ihren harmonischen Relationen," KONGRESS 1949 (Basel) 135–41.

424 Hammerschmidt, Andreas. From Preface to *Erster Fleiss,* ed. by H. Mönkemeyer, EdM XLIX (bowing).

425 Hammerstein, Reinhold. "Die Musik am Freiburger Münster; Ein Beitrag zur musikalischen Ikonographie," AfMw IX (1952) 204–18.

426 Handschin, Jacques. "Cembalo und Klavichord," SMZ LXX (1930) 133–41.

427 ——. "Das Pedalklavier," ZfMw XVII (1935) 418–25 (Renaissance and Baroque).

428 ——. "Réflexions dangereuses sur le renouveau de la musique ancienne," KONGRESS 1938 (Florence) 40–57.

428.01 Hansell, Sven Hostrup. "The Cadence in 18th-Century Recitative," MQ LIV (1968) 228–48.

429 Haraszti, Emile. "La technique des Improvisateurs de langue vulgaire et de latin au quattrocento," RB IX (1955) 12–31.

430 Harding, Rosamond Evelyn Mary. *Origins of Musical Time and Expression.* London: Oxford University Press, 1938 (incl. tempo, dynamics).

431 Harich-Schneider, Eta. "Hätte Bach. . . . (Missvertändnisse um das Cembalo)," Festschrift BACH-PROBLEME 67–69 (harpsichord—piano).

432 ——. *Die Kunst des Cembalo-Spiels. . . .* Kassel: Bärenreiter, [c. 1939]. Eng. trans. as *The Harpsichord: An Introduction to Technique, Style and the Historical Sources.* Kassel: Bärenreiter, 1954 (incl. touch,

48

fingering, articulation, ornamentation, tempo, registration, *b. c.*, and bibliography of sources).

433 ——. "Über die Angleichung nachschlagender Sechzehntel an Triolen," Mf XII (1959) 35–59 (*notes inégales*).

434 —— and Ricard Boadella. "Zum Klavichordspiel bei Tomàs de Santa Maria," AfMf II (1937) 243–45.

434.01 Harley, John. "The Trill in Beethoven's Later Music," MT XCV (1954) 69–73.

435 Harmans, Wilhelm. "Der ungeschriebene Gesangsvorschlag," Mk XIV/3 (1914–15) 162–76 (Baroque to Romantic).

436 *The Harpsichord Illustrated and Improv'd; Wherein is shewn the Italian Manner of Fingering.* . . . London: T. Cobb, [ca. 1736] (incl. ornamentation, fingering, *b. c.*, tuning). Also published as sixth part of *The Modern Musick Master* . . . (cf. **822.01**).

436.01 "Harpsichord Touch." Quotations from 18th-Century Writers, *The Consort* No. 6 (1949) 14–16.

437 Harrison, Frank Ll. "Tradition and Innovation in Instrumental Usage 1100–1450," Festschrift REESE 319–35.

438 Hartnack, Joachim W. "Das Recht des ausübenden Künstlers," unpublished Ph.D. diss., Rostock, 1946.

438.01 Harty, Hamilton. "Beethoven's Orchestra," ML VIII (1927) 172–77.

439 Haseke, Walter. "Untersuchungen zur Flötenspielpraxis des 18./19. Jahrhunderts. (Über die Flöte mit mehreren Klappen)," unpublished Ph.D. diss., Cologne, 1954.

440 Hasse, Karl. "Die Instrumentation J. S. Bachs," BJ XXVI (1929) 90–141 (make-up of groups).

441 ——. "Temperierte Stimmung und musikalische Praxis," ZfMw XIII (1930) 353–68 (equal temperament and mean-tone tuning).

441.01 Hastings, Thomas. *Dissertation on Musical Taste.* New York: Mason Brothers, 1853. Reprinted by Johnson Reprint Corp., 1968 (tone, articulation, expression, ornaments).

441.02 [——.] *The Musical Reader, or Practical Lessons for the Voice.* . . . Utica: William Williams, 1817 (incl. appoggiatura).

442 Havingha Gerhardus. From Preface to *Werken voor Clavicimbel*, ed. by E. Lemaire, MMB VII (incl. ornaments).

443 Hawkins, John Sidney. *An Inquiry into the Nature and Principles of Thorough Bass on a new plan.* . . . London: for the Author, by S. Gosnell, [1817].

444 Haydon, Glen. "On the Problem of Expression in Baroque Music," JAMS III (1950) 113–19.

445 Hayes, Gerald R. *Musical Instruments and their Music, 1500–1750*, 2 vols. London: Oxford University Press, 1928–30 (Vol. II includes bowed instruments).

446 Heartz, Daniel. "The Basse Dance. Its Evolution circa 1450 to 1550," AnnMl VI (1958–63) 287–340.

447 ——. "An Elizabethan Tutor for the Guitar," GSJ XVI (1963) 3–21 (incl. tuning, stringing, plucking).

448 ——. "Hoftanz and Basse Dance," JAMS XIX (1966) 13–36 (incl. instrumentation).

449 Heck, Johann Caspar. *The Art of Fingering.* . . . London: W. Randall & I. Abell, [ca. 1766–71] (incl. ornamentation).

450 ——. *The Art of Playing the Harpsichord.* London: [1770].

451 ——. *The Art of Playing Thorough Bass.* . . . London: John Welcher, [177–], and London: John Preston, [1793].

452 ——. *A Complete System of Harmony.* . . . London: Mssrs. Thompsons, [1768] (*b. c.*).

452.01 ——. *Short and fundamental instructions for learning thorough bass.* London: [n. p.], [177–].

453 Heckmann, Harald. "Der Takt in der Musiklehre des siebzehnten Jahrhunderts," AfMw X (1953) 116–39.

445 ——. "Zum Verhältnis von Musikforschung und Aufführungspraxis alter Musik," Mf X (1957) 98–107 (incl. bibliography).

455 Heinichen, Johann David. *Der General-Bass in der Composition.* . . . Dresden: Bey dem autore, 1728. Eng. trans. by G. J. Buelow as *Thorough-Bass Accompaniment According to Johann David Heinichen.* Berkeley: University of California Press, 1966 (incl. realizations).

456 Heinitz, Wilhelm. "Physiologische Beobachtungen zur Werk-Ästhetik F. Chopins," KONGRESS 1960 (Chopin) 433–37.

457 ——. "Taktprobleme in J. S. Bachs 'Wohltemperiertem Klavier,'" Festschrift SCHNEIDER (80) 147–51.

458 Heinrichs, Joseph. *Über den Sinn der Lisztschen Programmusik.* Kempen-Rh.: 1929.

459 Hellmann, Diethard. "Betrachtungen zur Darstellung der Sweelinck-schen Werke für Tasteninstrumente," MuK XXV (1955) 287–92 (organ vs. harpsichord).

460 Helm, Ernest Eugene. *Music at the Court of Frederick the Great.* Norman: University of Oklahoma Press, 1960 (incl. Quantz, C. P. E. and J. S. Bach, Marpurg, Kirnberger, *et al.*).

461 Hely, Benjamin. *The Compleat Violist.* . . . London: Printed for & sould by J. Hare, [ca. 1705] (incl. Psalm tunes).

462 Henking, Arwed. "Probleme des Rhythmus in Händels 'Messias,'" MuK XXXV (1965) 183–90 (dotted rhythm, *notes inégales*).

463 Herbst, Johann Andreas. *Musica practica sive instructio pro symphonia-cis.* . . . Nuremberg: Jeremiae Dümler, 1642. 2nd ed. as *Musica moderna prattica, overo maniera del buon canto.* . . . Frankfurt: Georg Müller, 1658 (title also: *Eine kurtze Anleitung* . . .) (incl. vocal ornamentation, improvisation, terms).

464 Hering, Hans. "Die Dynamik in Joh. Seb. Bachs Klaviermusik," BJ XXXVIII (1949–50) 65–80.

465 Heriot, Angus. *The Castrati in Opera*. London: Secker and Warburg, 1956.

466 Herrmann-Bengen, Irmgard. *Tempobezeichnungen: Ursprung-Wandel im 17. und 18. Jahrhundert*. Tutzing: H. Schneider, 1959.

467 Hertzmann, Erich. "Zur Frage der Mehrchörigkeit in der ersten Hälfte des 16. Jahrhunderts," ZfMw XII (1929–30) 138–47.

467.01 Hess, Joachim. *Korte en eenvoudige Handleyding tot het Leeren van t' Clavecimbel of Orgel-spel.* . . . Gouda: Johannes van der Klos, 1779 (incl. ornamentation, *b. c.*).

468 Hess, Willy. "Die Teilwiederholung in Beethovens Sinfoniesätzen," SMZ LXXXVIII (1948) 8–15.

469 ———. "Die Teilwiederholung in der Klassischen Sinfonie und Kammermusik," Mf XVI (1963) 238–52.

470 ———. "Zur Frage der Teilwiederholung in Beethovens Symphoniesätzen," Festschrift SCHMIDT-GÖRG (60) 142–55.

471 Hesse, Johann Heinrich. *Kurze, doch hinlängliche Anweisung zum General-Basse.* . . . Hamburg: M. C. Bock, [1776].

472 Heuss, Alfred. "Bachs Motetten, begleitet oder unbegleitet?" ZIMG VI (1904–1905) 107–13.

473 ———. "Die Dynamik der Mannheimer Schule. II. Die Detail-Dynamik, nebst einer dynamischen Analyse von Mozarts Andante aus der Mannheimer Sonate. K. 309," ZfMw II (1919) 44–54.

474 ———. "Das Orchester-Crescendo bei Beethoven," ZfMw IX (1926–27) 361–65.

475 ———. "Über die Dynamik der Mannheimer Schule," Festschrift RIEMANN 433–55 (cf. 473 *supra*).

476 ———. "Wie verhält es sich mit den Taktstrichen in dem Zauberflöten-Duett: Bei Männern, welche Liebe fühlen?" Festschrift ADLER 174–78 (accent, beat, measures).

476.001 ———. "Zum Thema Mannheimer Vorhalt," ZIMG IX (1907–1908) 273–80 (ornamentation, dynamics).

476.002 Heussner, Horst. "Zur Musizierpraxis der Klavierkonzerte im 18. Jahrhundert," Mozart Jb (1967) 165–75.

476.01 Heyde, Herbert. "Die Unterscheidung von Klarin- und Prinzipaltrompete," BzMw IX (1967) 55–61 (17–18th centuries; instrumentation).

477 Hiekel, Hans Otto. "'Tactus' und Tempo," KONGRESS 1962 (Kassel) 145–47.

477.01 Higbee, Dale. "Michel Corrette on the Piccolo and Speculations Regarding Vivaldi's 'Flautino,'" GSJ XVII (1964) 115–17.

477.02 ———. "A Plea for the Tenor Recorder by Thomas Stanesby, Jr.," GSJ XV (1962) 55–59.

477.03 ——. "Third-Octave Fingerings in the Eighteenth Century Recorder Charts," GSJ XV (1962) 97–99.

477.04 Higgins, Thomas. "Chopin Interpretation: A Study of Performance Practices in Selected Autographs and Other Sources," unpublished Ph.D. diss., University of Iowa, 1966.

478 Hillemann, Willi. "Auftreten und Verwendung der Blockflöte in den Werken Georg Friedrich Händels," Mf VIII (1955) 157–69 (incl. articulation, embellishment).

478.01 Hiller, Johann Adam. *Anweisung zum musikalisch-zierlichen Gesange.* Leipzig: Johann Friedrich Junius, 1780 (ornamentation, cadences, tone production, realized exx. of adagio).

478.02 ——. *Anweisung zum musikalisch-richtigen Gesange.* . . . Leipzig: Johann Friedrich Junius, 1774 (incl. ornaments).

479 ——. *Anweisung zum Violinspielen.* . . . Leipzig: Breitkopf, 1792 (incl. lexicon).

479.01 Hitchcock, H. Wiley (ed.). Preface to Marc-Antoine Charpentier's *Judicum Salomonis.* New Haven: A-R Editions, 1964 (orchestration, tempo, dynamics, accentuation).

479.02 Hizler, Daniel. *Extract aus der Neuen Musica oder Singkunst.* Nuremberg: Abraham Wagenmann, 1623 (esp. proportions, incl. lute tunings).

479.03 Hladky, Vinzenz and Maria Hinterberger. *Musik für die Mandoline: Anschlagsarten und Phrasierung; Die Verzierungen.* Wien: Musikverlag V. Hladky, 1955 (mainly charts).

480 Hoffmann, Adolf (ed.). Preface to Placidus Cajetanus Laurentius von Camerloher's *Drei Freisinger Sinfonien.* Wolfenbüttel: Moseler Verlag, 1956 (incl. dynamics, articulation, tempo, ornaments).

481 Hoffmann, Hans. "Aufführungspraxis," MGG I Col. 783–810 (incl. bibliography).

482 ——. "Vortragsschwierigkeiten bei Musik von Heinrich Schütz," MuK VI (1934) 19–32 (articulation and phrasing).

483 ——. "Zur Aufführungspraxis von Motteten alter Meister," MuK V (1933) 87–97 (number of performers, instrumentation, *b. c.,* a cappella question).

484 Hofmann, Richard. "Die F-Trompete im 2. Brandenburgischen Konzert von Joh. Seb. Bach," BJ XIII (1916) 1–7.

485 Holcman, Jan. *The Legacy of Chopin.* New York: Philosophical Library, 1954 (incl. Chopin's own comments).

486 Holder, William. *A Treatise of the Natural Grounds, and Principles of Harmony* . . . , [2nd ed.?]. London: Printed by W. Pearson for J. Wilcox, 1731 (incl. *b. c.,* tuning directions).

487 Holsinger, Clyde William. "A History of Choral Conducting with Emphasis on the Time-Beating Techniques Used . . . ," unpublished Ph.D. diss., Northwestern University, 1954.

488 Holst, Ortwin von. "Von der Problematik der Aufführungspraxis Bachscher Passionen," MuK XXXII (1962) 55–65.

489 Holzmann, Klaus. "Musikwissenschaft und Schallplatte," AfMw XII (1955) 88–95 ("Archiv-Produktion" of DGG).

490 Horn, Gitta. "La note pointée dans les œuvres pour clavecin de J. S. Bach," RMl XVI (1935) 27–33 (dotted notes).

491 Horn, Paul. "Studien zum Zeitmass in der Musik J. S. Bachs. Versuche über seine Kirchenliedbearbeitungen," unpublished Ph.D. diss., Tübingen, 1954.

492 Horsley, Imogene. "Improvised Embellishment in the Performance of Renaissance Polyphonic Music," JAMS IV (1951) 3–19 (vocal).

493 ——. "Wind Techniques in the Sixteenth and Early Seventeenth Centuries," BQ IV (1960–61) 49–63 (ornaments, articulation, technique).

493.01 Hotteterre, Jacques Martin. *Méthode pour la musette. . . . Op. 10.* Paris. J.-B.-Christophe Ballard, 1738 (incl. fingering, ornamentation).

494 ——. *Principes de la flute traversière, ou flute d'Allemagne; de la flute à bec, ou flute douce, et du haut-bois.* Paris: Christophe Ballard, 1707. Fac. and Ger. trans. of Amsterdam [1728] ed. by H. H. Hellwig. Kassel: Bärenreiter, 1958. Eng. trans. of 1st ed. by D. Lasocki as *Principles of the Flute, Recorder, and Oboe.* New York: Praeger, 1968.

495 Houle, George. "Tongueing and Rhythmic Patterns in Early Music," AR VI/2 (1965) 4–13.

496 Howell, Almonte C., Jr. (ed.). Preface to *Five French Baroque Organ Masses.* Lexington: University of Kentucky Press, 1961 (registration, ornaments, tempo).

496.01 Howerton, George Russell. "A Comparative Study of Performance Style in Choral Literature from the Renaissance to the Modern Period," unpublished Ph.D. diss., Northwestern University, 1950.

496.02 Howes, Frank. "The 'St. Matthew' Passion: Some Problems of Performance," MT LXXII (1931) 401–05 (*da capo, b. c.*).

497 Huber, Anna Gertrud. *Ludwig Van Beethoven, seine Schüler und Interpreten.* Vienna: Krieg, 1953 (instrumental music).

497.01 Hudgebut, John. *A Vade Mecum for the Lovers of Musick, Shewing the Excellency of the Rechorder. . . .* London: N. Thompson, 1678 (fingering, articulation).

497.02 Hudson, Barton. "Notes on Gregorio Strozzi and his *Capricci*," JAMS XX (1967) 209–21 (ornamentation).

498 Hughes, Andrew. "Mensural Polyphony for Choir in 15th-Century England," JAMS XIX (1966) 352–69 (choir or solo).

498.01 Hughes, Edwin. "The 'Forty-Eight' from the Player's Standpoint," MQ XI (1925) 444–53 (piano-clavichord question).

498.02 Hughes, Rosemary. "The Haydn Orchestra," MT XCIII (1952) 299–301.

499 Hummel, Johann Nepomuk. *Ausführliche theoretisch-practische Anweisung zum Piano-Forte-Spiel.* Vienna: T. Haslinger, 1828.

499.01 ——. "On Extemporaneous Performance," MMR XI (1881) 241–51 (19th century).

500 Husmann, Heinrich. "Die 'Kunst der Fuge' als Klavierwerk. Besetzung und Anordnung," BJ XXXV (1938) 1–61.

501 ——. "Die viola pomposa," BJ XXXIII (1936) 90–100 (in Bach).

501.01 ——. "Zur Charakteristik der Schlickschen Temperatur," AfMw XXIV (1967) 253–65.

502 Hutchings, Arthur. "The English Concerto with or for Organ," MQ XLVII (1961) 195–206 (if and when used).

502.01 Hutchins, Farley K. *Dietrich Buxtehude: The Man, His Music, His Era.* Paterson: Music Textbook Co., 1955 (incl. fingering, articulation).

I

503 Isler, Ernst. "Georg Friedrich Händels Orgelkonzerte," SMZ LXXXIV (1944) 309–18, 351–56 (Handel's registrations).

J

504 Jackson, George K. *A Treatise on Practical Thorough Bass, with General Rules for its Composition & Modulation . . . Op. 5.* London: Longman & Broderip, [1795?].

505 Jackson, William. *Observations on the Present State of Music in London.* Dublin: A. Grueber, 1791, and London: Harrison and Co., 1791 (comprehensive).

505.01 Jacobi, Erwin R. "G. F. Nicolai's Manuscript of Tartini's *Regole per ben suonar il Violino*," MQ XLVII (1961) 207–23.

506 ——. "Neues zur Frage 'Punktierte Rhythmen gegen Triolen' und zur Transkriptionstechnik bei J. S. Bach," BJ XLIX (1962) 88–96 (*notes inégales*).

507 ——. "Über die Angleichung nachschlagender Sechzehntel an Triolen," Mf XIII (1960) 268–81 (*notes inégales*, incl. bibliography) (cf. Harich-Schneider, "Über die Angleichung . . .").

508 Jacobs, Charles Gilbert. "The Performance Practice of Spanish Renaissance Keyboard Music," 2 vols., unpublished Ph.D. diss., New York University, 1962.

508.01 Jaenike, Margrit. *"Arte Antica:" Von der Erkenntnis und Darstellung der Lebendigkeit alter Musik.* Zurich: Kommissionsverlag Hug & Co., [1938].

508.02 Jander, Owen. "Concerto Grosso Instrumentation in Rome in the 1600's and 1700's," JAMS XXI (1968) 168–80.

509 Jansen, Martin. "Cembalo in Bachs Matthäuspassion?" MuK VIII (1936) 127–29 (cf. Müller, F., "Darf man . . .").

509.01 Jenne, Natalie. "Some Suggestions for the Performance of Merulo's Toccatas," *The Diapason* (May 1968) 32–33 (rhythm, tempo, ornamentation, fingerings, organ or harpsichord).

510 Jeppesen, Knud. "Palestrina e l'interpretazione," KONGRESS 1938 (Florence) 166–72.

510.01 Johnson, Jane Troy. "How to 'Humour' John Jenkins' Three-part Dances: Performance Directions in a Newberry Library MS," JAMS XX (1967) 197–208.

511 Johnstone, H. Diack. "Tempi in Corelli's Christmas Concerto," MT CVII (1966) 956–59.

512 Jonas, Oswald. "Bemerkungen zu Beethovens Op. 96," AM1 XXXVII (1965) 87–89.

512.01 ———. "Improvisation in Mozarts Klavierwerken," Mozart Jb (1967) 176–81.

513 Jullien, Gilles. Preface to *Premier Livre d'Orgue*, PSFM Ser. 1, Vol. XIII (incl. table of ornaments).

514 Jung, Hans Rudolf. "Ein unbekanntes Gutachten von Heinrich Schütz," BzMw IV (1962) 17–36.

515 Jurisch, Herta. "Prinzipien der Dynamik im Klavierwerk Philipp Emanuel Bachs," unpublished Ph.D. diss., Tübingen, 1959.

516 ———. "Zur Dynamik im Klavierwerk Ph.E. Bachs," KONGRESS 1962 (Kassel) 178–81.

K

517 Kämper, Dietrich. "Zur Frage der Metronombezeichnungen Robert Schumanns," AfMw XXI (1964) 141–55.

518 Kahl, Willi. "Frühe Lehrwerke für das Hammerklavier," AfMw IX (1952) 231–45 (comparison of piano and clavichord techniques).

518.01 Kalix, Adalbert. *Studien über die Wiedergabe romantischer Musik in der Gegenwart an Schallplatten-Aufnahmen der Freischütz-Ouverture C. M. v. Webers.* Nuremberg: Fritz Osterchrist, 1934 (conducting, tempo).

519 Kamieński, Lucian. *Die Oratorien von Johann Adolf Hasse.* Leipzig: Breitkopf & Härtel, 1912 (esp. Chapter 4).

520 ———. "Zum 'Tempo Rubato,'" AfMw I (1918–19) 108–26.

521 Kański, Józef. "Über die Aufführungsstile der Werke Chopins," KONGRESS 1960 (Chopin) 444–48 (tempo).

521.01 Kapsberger, Johann Hieronymus von. *Libro primo di arie passeggiate.* . . . [Rome:] 1612 (Vol. II pub. 1623) (ornamentation).

521.02 ———. *Libro primo di motetti passeggiati.* . . . Rome: Francesco de Nobili, 1612 (written-out diminutions).

522 Karstädt, Georg. "Aufführungspraktische Fragen bei Verwendung von Naturtrompeten, Naturhörnern und Zinken," KONGRESS 1953 (Bamberg) 93–95.

523 ——. "Horn und Zink bei Johann Sebastian Bach," MuK XXII (1952) 187–90.

524 ——. "Zur Geschichte des Zinken und seiner Verwendung in der Musik des 16. bis 18. Jahrhunderts," AfMf II (1937) 385–432.

525 Kastner, Santiago. "Le 'clavecin parfait' de Bartolomeo Jobernardi," AnM VIII (1953) 193–209 (partial translation into French of Jobernardi's *Tratado de la Música*).

526 ——. "Harfe und Harfner in der Iberischen Musik des 17. Jahrhunderts," *Natalicia musicologica Knud Jeppesen septuagenario collegis oblata*, ed. by B. Hjelmborg & S. Sørensen. Copenhagen: Wilhelm Hansen, 1962 165–72.

527 —— (ed.). Preface to P. Antonio Soler's *2 × 2 Sonatas*. Mainz: B. Schott, 1956 (ornaments, articulation, extemporization).

528 Kehr, Heinz-Günther. "Untersuchungen zur Violintechnik um die Wende des 18. Jahrhunderts. Ein Beitrag zur Entwicklungsgeschichte des Violinspiels," unpublished Ph.D. diss., Cologne, 1941 (incl. bowing).

529 Keller, Gottfried. *A Compleat Method, for Attaining to Play a Through Bass upon either Organ, Harpsichord or Theorbo Lute.* . . . London: R. Meares, [1721]. Also in William Holder, *A Treatise of the Natural Grounds and Principles of Harmony*. London: W. Pearson, 1731.

530 Keller, Hermann. *Domenico Scarlatti: Ein Meister des Klaviers*. Leipzig: C. F. Peters, 1957 (ornamentation, articulation, tempo, and echo technique).

531 ——. *Die Klavierwerke Bachs: Ein Beitrag zu ihrer Geschichte, Form, Deutung und Wiedergabe*. Leipzig: C. F. Peters, 1950.

532 ——. *Die musikalische Artikulation, inbesondere bei Joh. Seb. Bach. Mit 342 Notenbeispielen und einem Anhang: Versuch einer Artikulation der Fugenthemen des Wohltemperierten Klaviers und der Orgelwerke*. Stuttgart: Schultheiss, 1925 (incl. Mozart).

532.01 ——. *The Organ Works of Bach: A Contribution to their History, Form, Interpretation and Performance*, trans. by Helen Hewitt. New York: C. F. Peters Corp., 1967 (incl. registration, dynamics, tempo, ornamentation, phrasing, articulation).

532.02 ——. "Ornamentik—einmal anders gesehen," NZfM CXVII (1956) 611–14.

533 ——. *Phrasierung und Artikulation*. Kassel: Bärenreiter, 1955. Eng. trans. by L. Gerdine as *Phrasing and Articulation*. New York: W. W. Norton, 1965.

534 ——. *Schule des Generalbassspiels* . . . , 2nd ed. Kassel: Bärenreiter, 1950. Eng. trans. by C. Parrish as *Thoroughbass Method*. New York: W. W. Norton, 1965 (quotes Praetorius, Niedt, Telemann,

Matheson, Heinichen, J. S. and Ph. E. Bach, Quantz, Padre Mattei).

535 ——. "Das Tempo bei Bach," *Neue Musikzeitschrift* IV (1950) 125–27.

536 Kelletat, Herbert. "Grundlagen der Orgeltechnik," MuK VI (1934) 121–27 (incl. phrasing, articulation, touch, fingering).

536.01 Kellner, David. *Korte en getrouwe onderregtinge van de generaal bass, of bassus continuus.* Amsterdam: G. F. Witvogel, 1741.

537 ——. *Treulicher Unterricht im Generalbass,* 2nd ed. Hamburg: C. Herold, 1737.

538 Kellner, Johann Christoph. *Grundriss des Generalbasses . . . Op. XVI,* Pt. 1. Kassel: bedrückt auf Kosten der Verfassers, [17—].

538.01 Kelly, Cuthbert. "Madrigals from a Singer's Point of View," ML XII (1931) 232–41.

539 Kendall, Raymond. "Notes on Arnold Schlick," AM1 XI (1939) 136–43 (organ tunings).

540 Kennard, Francis. "Handel and His Favorite Keys," *Musical Opinion* LXXIII (1950) 106–116.

541 Kessel, Johann Christian Bertram. *Unterricht im Generalbasse zum gebrauche für Lehrer und Lernende,* new ed. Leipzig: C. G. Hertel, 1791.

542 Kienle, P. Ambrosius. "Notizen über das Dirigiren mittelalterlicher Gesangschöre," VfMw I (1885) 158–69.

542.001 Kind, Silvia. "Barocke Cembalo-Musik," NZfM CXXVIII (1967) 317–19 (esp. rhythm).

542.01 King, Alexander Hyatt. "Mozart and the Organ," and "The Clavier in Mozart's Life," *Mozart in Retrospect.* London: Oxford University Press, 1955 228–41, 242–59.

542.02 ——. "Mozart Manuscripts at Cambridge," MR II (1941) 29–35 (K. 497, 521, 593; expression, trills, staccato).

543 Kinkeldey, Otto. "Bach embellecido por sí mismo," *Revista de Estudios Musicales* III (1954) 271–80.

544 ——. *Orgel und Klavier in der Musik des 16. Jahrhunderts.* Leipzig: Breitkopf & Härtel, 1910.

545 Kinsky, Georg. "Pedalklavier oder Orgel bei Bach?" AM1 VIII (1936) 158–61.

546 Kirby, F. E. "Hermann Finck on Methods of Performance," ML XLII (1961) 212–20.

547 Kirchner, Gerhard. *Der Generalbass bei Heinrich Schütz.* Kassel: Bärenreiter, 1960.

548 Kirkpatrick, Ralph. "Eighteenth-Century Metronomic Indications," AMS Papers (1938) 30–50.

549 ——. "The Performance of the Scarlatti Sonatas," and "Ornamentation in Scarlatti," *Domenico Scarlatti.* Princeton: Princeton University Press, 1953 280–323, 365–98.

550 —— (ed.). Preface to J. S. Bach's *Goldberg Variations*. New York: G. Schirmer, [1938] (incl. ornaments, fingering, phrasing, tempo, dynamics).

551 Kirnberger, Johann Philipp. *Grundsätze des Generalbasses als erste Linien zur Composition.* Berlin: J. J. Hummel, [1781] (realizations).

552 ——. *Die Kunst des reinen Satzes in der Musik* . . . , 2 vols. Berlin: G. J. Decker & G. L. Hartung, 1774–79 (incl. *b. c.*).

552.01 Kitchiner, William. *Observations on Vocal Music.* London: Hurst, Robinson, and Co., 1821 (articulation, accents, esp. of solo music).

553 Kittel, Johann Christian. *Der angehende praktische Organist* . . . , 3 vols. in 1. Erfurt: Beyer and Maring, 1808 (chorale preludes and chorale improvisation).

554 ——. "Noter-Buch Dal Signor Kittell," MS Library of Congress, MT224.K62 Case [c. 1789?] (incl. ornamentation, fingering).

554.01 Kleczyński, Jean. *Frédéric Chopin. De l'interprétation de ses oeuvres.* Paris: Fischbacher, 1880 (incl. fingering, ornamentation, articulation).

554.02 Klee, Ludwig. *Die Ornamentik der Klassischer Klavier-Musik.* Leipzig: Breitkopf & Härtel, [18—].

555 Klein, Johann Joseph. *Lehrbuch der theoretischen Musik in systematischer Ordnung entworfen.* Leipzig and Gera: Wilhelm Heinsius, 1801 (incl. tuning, articulation).

556 Klein, Rudolf. "Ein Bildzeugnis aus dem 16. Jahrhundert," Österr MZ XV (1960) 140–43.

557 ——. "Der neue alte Orgelstil," Österr MZ V (1950) 106–14 (phrasing and articulation in Bach).

558 Klenz, William, *Giovanni Maria Bononcini: A Chapter in Baroque Instrumental Music.* Durham: Duke University Press, 1962 (esp. dances, "letters to reader").

559 Kloppers, Jacobus. "Die Interpretation und Wiedergabe der Orgelwerke Bachs," unpublished Ph.D. diss., Frankfurt am Main, 1965.

560 Klotz, Hans. "Comment Bach interprétait Bach," *La Revue Internationale de Musique* VIII (1950) 68–79 (organ tempo, expression).

561 ——. "Johann Sebastian Bach und die Orgel," MuK XXXII (1962) 49–55 (incl. registration, articulation, tempo).

562 ——. "Die Registrierkunst der Französischen Organisten des 17. und 18. Jahrhunderts und das Bachspiel," KONGRESS 1949 (Basel) 172–76.

563 ——. "Zur Registrierkunst in der klassischen Zeit des Orgelspiels," MuK II (1930) 80–87, 103–11.

564 Knecht, Justin Heinrich. *Bewährtes Methodenbuch beim ersten Klavierunterricht.* . . . Freiburg: Herder, [1825] (incl. *b. c.*).

565 ———. *Kleine theoretische Klavierschule* . . ., Pt. 2. Munich: Falter, [1800–1802] (incl. fingering, ornamentation, accents).

566 ———. *Theoretisch-praktische Generalbassschule.* . . . Freiburg: Herder, [1825] (Pt. 2 contains realizations).

566.01 ———. *Vollständige Orgelschule für Anfänger und Geübtere*, 3 vols. Leipzig: Breitkopf & Härtel, [1795–98].

567 Knödt, Heinrich. "Die Konzertkadenz," unpublished Ph.D. diss., Vienna, 1911 (piano, Classic).

568 Koch, Caspar. *The Organ Student's Gradus ad Parnassum.* New York: J. Fischer, 1945 (esp. Bach).

569 Koch, Johannes H. E. "Vorübungen zur Improvisation auf der Orgel," *Kirchenmusik, Vermächtnis und Aufgabe, 1948–1958*; *Festschrift zum zehnjährigen Bestehen der westfälischen Landeskirchenmusikschule in Herford*, ed. by W. Ehmann. Darmstadt-Eberstadt: K. Merseburger, [1958?] 86–99.

570 Kock-Concepción, Hermann. "Bachs Artikulation," MuK XXIII (1953) 65–69.

571 Koczirz, Adolf. "Eine Titelauflage aus dem Jahre 1697 von Esaias Reussners 'Erfreuliche Lauten-Lust,'" ZfMw VIII (1925–26) 636–40 (fingering and technique).

572 ——— (ed.). Preface to *Österreichische Lautenmusik zwischen 1650 und 1720*, DTÖ (tuning and hand position).

573 Köhler, Werner Eginhard. *Beiträge zur Geschichte und Literatur der Viola d'amore.* Berlin: Funk, [1938] (incl. bibliography).

574 Köppel, Robert. "Die Paraphrase. Ein Beitrag zur Geschichte der virtuosen Klaviertechnik," unpublished Ph.D. diss., Vienna, 1936.

575 Körte, Oswald. *Laute und Lautenmusik bis zur Mitte des 16. Jahrhunderts*, (PIMG III). Leipzig: Breitkopf & Härtel, 1901 1–162 (incl. tuning, ornamentation, style).

576 Kolisch, Rudolf. "Tempo and Character in Beethoven's Music," MQ XXIX (1943) 169–87, 291–312.

576.01 Kollmann, August Friedrich Christoph. *An Introduction to the Art of Preluding and Extemporizing* . . . *for the Harpsichord or Harp.* London: R. Wornum, [179–?].

577 ———. *A Practical Guide to Thorough-Bass.* London: for the Author, 1801 (incl. realizations).

578 "Kolloquium über aufführungspraktische Fragen bei Händel," Händel Jb (1966) 25–49.

579 Kolneder, Walter. *Aufführungspraxis bei Vivaldi.* Leipzig: Breitkopf & Härtel, 1955.

580 ———. "Der Aufführungsstil Vivaldis," Österr MZ XIX (1964) 574–78 (Vivaldi's conducting and interpretation as violinist).

581 Krabbe, Wilhelm (ed.). Preface to Georg Philipp Telemann's

59

Vierundzwanzig Oden, and Johann Valentin Görner's *Sammlung neuer Oden und Lieder*, DDT LVII (rhythm).

582 Kramolisch, Walter (ed.). "Die Quellen" *in* Johann Schobert's *Sechs Sinfonien für Cembalo mit Begleitung von Violine und Hörnern ad libitum*, EdM, Sub. Ser. I, Vol. IV (ornamentation).

583 Krause, Joachim. "Dietrich Buxtehudes 'Singet dem Herrn': Ein Vorschlag zur Aufführungspraxis," MuK XXXIII (1963) 165–70 (incl. tempo, *b. c.*).

583.01 ——. "Von Klingenden Kreuzzeichen," MuK XXXVII (1967) 207–15 (articulation and expression in 18th-century organ music, esp. J. S. Bach).

583.02 Krebs, Carl. "Girolamo Diruta's *Transilvano*. Ein Beitrag zur Geschichte des Orgel- und- Klavierspiels im 16. Jahrhundert," VfMw VIII (1892) 307–88 (cf. **257**).

584 Kretzschmar, Hermann. "Einige Bemerkungen über den Vortrag alter Musik," JbP VII (1900) 51–68 (instrumentation, dynamics, phrasing).

584.01 Kreutz, Alfred (ed.). *Die Ornamentik in J. S. Bach's Klavier-Werken*, supp. to Urtext ed. of *English Suites*. Frankfurt: C. F. Peters, [ca. 1951].

585 Krey, Johannes. "Zur Bedeutung der Fermaten in Bachs Chorälen," BJ XLIII (1956) 105–11.

586 Kroyer, Theodor. "A cappella oder Conserto?" *Festschrift Hermann Kretzschmar zum siebzigsten Geburtstage überreicht von Kollegen, Schülern und Freunden*. Leipzig: C. F. Peters, 1918 65–73.

587 ——. "Dialog und Echo in der alten Chormusik," JbP XVI (1909) 13–32 (dynamics).

588 ——. "Zur A cappella-Frage," AfMw II (1919) 48–53.

589 Krüger, Hans. "Die Verstimmung (scordatura, discordatura) auf Saiten-Instrumenten in Beziehung zur klangen Einrichtung der Instrumente und zum Tonsystem und ihre Folgen auf die Aufführungspraxis," KONGRESS 1958 (Cologne) 172–74.

590 Krüger. Walther. "Aufführungspraktische Fragen mittelalterlicher Mehrstimmigkeit," Mf IX (1956) 419–27; X (1957) 279–86, 397–403, 497–505; XI (1958) 177–89.

590.01 Kürzinger, Ignatz Franz Xaver. *Getreuer Unterricht zum Singen mit Manieren, und die Violin zu Spielen*. . . . Augsburg: Johann Jacob Lotter, 1763 (incl. ornamentation).

591 Kuhlo, Franz. "Über melodische Verzierungen in der Tonkunst," unpublished Ph.D. diss., Berlin, 1896 (Baroque).

592 Kuhn, Max. *Die Verzierungs-Kunst in der Gesangs-Musik des 16.–17. Jahrhunderts (1535–1650)*, (PIMG VII). Leipzig: Breitkopf & Härtel, 1902 1–150 (principally Italian).

593 Kuhnau, Johann. Preface to *Nouvel Exercice pour le Clavecin, Le Trésor des Pianistes* X (incl. ornaments).

594 Kulenkampff, Georg. "Bachs Chaconne für Violine alleine," SMZ LXXXIX (1949) 457–69.

595 Kullak, Franz. *Beethoven's Piano Playing, with an Essay on the Execution of the Trill,* trans. by T. Baker. New York: G. Schirmer, 1901.

596 Kunze, Stefan. "Die Entstehung des Concertoprinzips im Spätwerk Giovanni Gabrielis," AfMw XXI (1964) 81–105.

597 Kusser, Johann Sigismund. *Composition de musique suivant la méthode française.* . . . Stuttgart: P. Treu, 1682.

L

598 Laag, Henrich. *Anfangsgründe zum Clavierspielen und Generalbas.* Osnabrück: bei Johann Wilhelm Schmid, 1774.

598.01 Lacassagne, Joseph. *Traité général des élémens du chant.* Paris: l'Auteur, 1766 (incl. ornaments).

599 Lach, Robert. *Studien zur Entwicklungsgeschichte der ornamentalen Melopöie.* Leipzig: C. F. Kahnt Nachfolger, 1913.

600 Lacroix, Yves. "L'Orchestre des électeurs de Trèves au XVIIIᵉ siècle," RM (Nov., 1927) 38–42, (Dec., 1927) 130–35 (size and repertoire; also choir).

600.01 L'Affillard, Michel. *Principes très-faciles pour bien apprendre la Musique.* . . . Paris: C. Ballard, 1694 (incl. ornamentation).

601 La Laurencie, Lionel de. *L'École française de violon de Lully à Viotti,* 3 vols. Paris: Delagrave, 1922–24 (17th and 18th centuries).

602 ——. "Un Maître de luth au XVIIᵉ siècle," RM (July, 1923) 224–37 (ornamentation, tempo, accents, scordatura).

603 ——. "Un primitif français du violon: Du Val," Mm I (1905) 59–72 (rhythm, arpeggios).

603.01 Lambert, Arthur Adams. "The Keyboard Partitas of J. S. Bach. A Study of Background, Text, and Interpretation," unpublished Ph.D. diss., State University of Iowa, 1961 (textual variants between editions, interpretation of text, harpsichord registration).

604 Lampe, John Frederick. *A Plain and Compendious Method of Teaching Thorough Bass.* . . . London: J. Wilcox, 1737.

605 Lampl, Hans. "Michael Praetorius on the Use of Trumpets," BQ II (1958–59) 3–8 (*Syntagma Musicum,* ch. 8).

606 Landau, Hela. "Die Neuerungen der Klaviertechnik bei Franz Liszt," unpublished Ph.D. diss., Vienna, 1933.

607 Landon, H. C. Robbins (ed.). Preface to Franz Joseph Haydn's *Collected Symphonies, 1–49.* Vienna: Doblinger, 1962 (instrumentation, articulation).

607.01 Landowska, Wanda. "Bach und die französische Klaviermusik," BJ VII (1910) 33–44 (ornamentation, rhythm).

608 ——. "Chopin und die alte französische Musik," Mk XXIV (1932) 484–91 (similarities between Chopin and French clavecinists).

609 ——. "En vue de quel instrument Bach a-t-il composé son *Wohltemperiertes Clavier?*" RM (Dec., 1927) 123–29.

610 ——. *Music of the Past,* trans. by W. A. Bradley. New York: Alfred Knopf, 1924 (incl. ornaments, sonority, harpsichord).

611 Landshoff, Ludwig. "Aufführungspraxis Bachscher Chorwerke," Mk XXI (1928) 81–97 (incl. instrumentation, dynamics, tempo, articulation).

612 ——. "Über das vielstimmige Accompagnement und andere Fragen des Generalbassspiels," Festschrift SANDBERGER 189–208 (quotes Gasparini, Geminiani, C. P. E. Bach, *et al.*).

613 Langlé, Honoré François Marie. *Nouvelle méthode pour chiffrer les accords.* Paris: Chez tous les marchands de musique, 1801.

614 ——. *Traité de la basse sous le chant.* . . . Paris: Naderman, [1798].

615 Langner, Thomas-Martin. "Darstellungs- und ausdrucksbetonte Werkbilder," *Musikerkenntnis und Musikerziehung: Dankesgaben für Hans Mersmann zu seinem 65. Geburtstage,* ed. by W. Wiora. Kassel: Bärenreiter, 1958 83–90 (expression).

616 ——. "Studien zur Dynamik Max Regers," unpublished Ph.D. diss., Berlin, 1953.

617 Laporte, Charles Nicolas de. *Traité théorique et pratique de l'accompagnement du clavecin.* . . . Paris: L'auteur, [17—].

617.01 Lasser, Johann Baptist. *Vollständige Anleitung zur Singkunst, sowohl für die Sopran, als auch für den Alt.* Munich: der Verfasser, 1798 (ornaments, recitative, arias, cadences, tempo).

618 Launay, Denise. "Les motets à double choeur en France dans la Iʳᵉ moitie du XVIIᵉ siècle," RMl XL (1957) 173–95 (size of chorus).

618.01 Lawrence, William John. "The English Theatre Orchestra: Its Rise and Early Characteristics," MQ III (1917) 9–27 (esp. seating).

619 Le Blanc, Hubert. *Defense de la basse de viole contre les entréprises du violon et les prétentions du violoncel.* Amsterdam: P. Mortier, 1740. Also: RM (Nov., 1927) 43–56, (Dec., 1927) 136–42, (Jan., 1928) 247–51, (Feb., 1928) 21–25, (Mar., 1928) 138–42, (June, 1928) 187–92 (viola da gamba).

620 [Le Cerf de La Vieville, Jean-Laurent]. *Comparaison de la musique italienne et de la musique françoise,* 3 vols in 1. Brussels: F. Foppens, 1704–06. Reprinted as vols. 2–4 of Jacques Bonnet's *Histoire de la Musique.* . . . Amsterdam: C. Le Cene, 1726 (French vs. Italian opera) (cf. Raguenet, *Parallele* . . .).

620.01 Le Huray, Peter. "Some Performance Problems," *Music and the Reformation in England 1549–1660.* New York: Oxford University

Press, 1967 90–134 (incl. sources, text underlay, pitch, accompaniment, vocal timbre, expression).

621 Leichtentritt, Hugo. "Einige Bemerkungen über Verwendung der Instrumente im Zeitalter Josquin's," ZIMG XIV (1912–13) 359–65 (criticism of Arnold Schering's *Die niederländische Orgelmesse im Zeitalter des Josquin*) (cf. Schering, "Zur 'Orgelmesse' . . ." and Leichtentritt, "Zur 'Orgelmesse' . . .").

622 —— (ed.). Preface to Andreas Hammerschmidt's *Ausgewählte Werke*, DDT XL (quotes Hammerschmidt's *Musikalischen Andachten* [1646] on bowing and slurring, also *b. c.*).

623 ——. "Über Pflege alter Vokalmusik," ZIMG VI (1904–1905) 192–202 (incl. tempo, dynamics, meter).

624 ——. "Zur 'Orgelmesse.' Duplik zu A. Schering's Ausführungen," ZIMG XV (1913–14) 17 (cf. Leichtentritt, "Eine Bemerkungen . . ." and Schering, "Zur 'Orgelmesse' . . .").

624.01 ——. "Zur Vortragspraxis des 17. Jahrhunderts," *Haydnzentenarfeier III. Kongress der Internationalen Musikgesellschaft Wien, 25. bis 29. Mai 1909*, ed. by G. Adler. Wien: Artaria, 1909 (incl. *b. c.*).

625 Leifs, Jon. "Interpretationsstudien," Neues Beethoven Jb III (1927) 62–90 (Third Symphony: Trauermarsch and Finale).

626 Lemoine, Micheline. "La technique violonistique de Jean-Marie Leclair," RM No. 226 (1955) 117–43.

626.01 Leonhardt, Gustav M. *The Art of Fugue: Bach's Last Harpsichord Work.* The Hague: M. Nijhoff, 1952 (scoring).

626.02 Lichtenthal, Herbert. "Musical Interpretation," MR IV (1943) 163–70 (esp. Bach, Beethoven, Brahms).

627 Llorens, José M. "Cristóbal de Morales, cantor en la Capilla Pontificia de Paulo III (1535–45)," AnM VIII (1953) 39–69 (incl. performers at papal chapel).

627.01 Lobe, Johann Christian. "Bach's Organ Compositions and their Treatment," MMR II (1881) 185–87 (technique).

628 Locke, Matthew. *Melothesia: Or Certain General Rules for Playing upon a Continued-Bass.* London: Printed for J. Carr, 1673.

629 Lockspeiser, Edward. "French Influences on Bach," ML XVI (1935) 312–20 (*willkürliche manieren*, ornamentation).

630 Löhlein, Georg Simon. *Anweisung zum Violinspielen.* . . . Leipzig and Züllichau: auf Kosten der Waysenhaus und Frommannischen Buchhandlung, 1774 (incl. fingering, ornamentation).

631 ——. *Clavier-Schule.* . . . Leipzig & Züllichau: auf Kosten der Waysenhaus und Frommanischen Buchhandlung, 1773 (incl. *b. c.*, ornamentation).

632 Löhrer, Edwin, and Otto Ursprung. Anmerkungen to Ludwig Senfl's *Sieben Messen zu vier bis sechs Stimmen*, EdM V (choir vs. solo, ornamentation).

633 Loeillet, Jean-Baptiste. Preface to *Werken voor Clavecimbal*, MMB I (incl. "Lessons for the Harpsichord . . .," ornaments).

634 Lohmann, Paul. "Das Legato der deutschen Sängers", Festschrift RAABE 182–86 (ca. 1800).

635 Longyear, Rey M. "Some Aspects of 16th-Century Instrumental Terminology and Practice," JAMS XVII (1964) 193–98.

635.001 Loonsma, Stephan Theodor van. *Muzicaal A, B,—Boek.* . . . Amsterdam: A. Olofsen, 1741 (keyboard, general).

635.002 Lopez Remacha, Miguel. *Arte de cantar, y compendio de documentos músicos respectivos al canto.* Madrid: Don Benito Cano, 1799 (comprehensive, esp. ornamentation, expression, pronunciation, recitative, solo voice and choral).

635.01 Lorenzoni, Antonio. *Saggio per ben sonare il flautotraverso.* Vicenza: Francesco Modena, 1779 (incl. ornamentation).

635.02 Lorince, Frank. "A Study of Musical Texture in Relation to Sonata-Form as Evidenced in Selected Keyboard Sonatas from C. P. E. Bach Through Beethoven," unpublished Ph.D. diss., University of Rochester, 1966.

635.03 Loud, Thomas. *The Organ Study*: . . . Philadelphia: Loud's Pianoforte & Music Store, 1845 (19th-century Americana, incl. registration of specific pieces).

636 Lowinsky, Edward. "Zur Frage der deklamations Rhythmik in der a-cappella-Musik des 16. Jahrhunderts," AMl VII (1935) 62–67 (text-rhythm).

637 Lungershausen, Hellmuth. "Zur instrumentalen Kolorierungspraxis des 18. Jahrhunderts," ZfMw XVI (1934) 513–26 (style galant).

638 Luntz, Erwin (ed.). Preface to Heinrich Franz Biber's *Sechzehn Violinsonaten*, DTÖ XXV (incl. scordatura).

638.01 Luoma, Robert Gust. "Francesco Durante's *Oratio Jeremiae Prophetae*: A Study in the Relationship Between Style, Structure and Performance," unpublished D. M. A. diss., Stanford University, 1967.

M

639 Mace, Thomas. *Musick's Monument.* . . . London: Printed by T. Radcliffe and N. Thompson, for the author, 1676. Fac. ed. by J. Jacquot and A. Souris, 2 vols. Paris: Éditions du Centre national de la recherche scientifique, 1958 (esp. singing, lute, viol).

640 Machatius, Franz-Jochen. "Die Tempi in der Musik um 1600," unpublished Ph.D. diss., Berlin, 1954.

641 ——. "Die Tempo-Charaktere," KONGRESS 1958 (Cologne) 185–87.

642 Mackerras, Charles. "Sense about the Appoggiatura," *Opera* XIV (1963) 669–78.

642.01 Mackerras, Joan. "Problems of Violin Bowing in the Performance of 18th-Century Music," *Canon* XVII/3 (1965) 25–30.

643 [Maffei, Giovanni Camillo]. *Delle Lettere del/S.ᵒʳ Giov. Camillo/Maffei da Solofra/Libri Due.* Naples: Raymundo Amato, 1562 (singing) (cf. Bridgman, "Giovanni Camillo Maffei . . .").

643.01 Mahaut, A. *Nieuwe Manier om binnen kortentyd op de Dwarsfluit te leeren speelen.* . . . 2nd ed. Amsterdam: J. J. Hummel, [n. d.] 1st. ed., 1759 (ornaments, articulation).

643.02 Mahling, Christoph-Hellmut. "Mozart und die Orchesterpraxis seiner Zeit," Mozart Jb (1967) 229–43.

644 Mahling, Friedrich. "Beethovens 'Missa Solemnis' im Erlebnis eines deutschen Malers der Gegenwart," Festschrift STEIN 33–47.

645 Mahrenholz, Christhard. "Samuel Scheidt und die Orgel," MuK XXV (1955) 38–50 (registrations).

646 Majer, Joseph Friedrich Bernhard Caspar. *Museum musicum theoretico practicum.* . . . Hall: Georg Michael Majer, 1732. Also as *Neu-eröffneter theoretisch- und praktischer music-saal.* . . . Nuremburg: J. J. Cremer, 1741. Fac. ed. by H. Becker. Kassel: Bärenreiter-Verlag, 1954.

647 Malvezzi, Christofano. Preface to *Intermedii et Concerti (1591).* VogelB I 382–85 (vocal).

648 Mancini, Giovanni Battista. *Pensieri, e riflessioni pratiche sopra il canto figurato.* Vienna: Stamparia di Ghelen, 1774. Trans. and ed. by E. Foreman as *Practical Reflections on Figured Singing.* Champaign: Pro Musica Press, 1968 (incl. figuration).

649 Manfredini, Vincenzo. *Regole armoniche.* . . . Venice: Appresso G. Zerletti, 1775 (*b. c.*).

650 Mantel, Georg. "Zur Ausführung der Arpeggien in J. S. Bachs 'Chromatischer Phantasie,'" BJ XXVI (1929) 142–52.

651 Marcello, Benedetto. "Il Teatro Alla Moda," trans. by R. G. Pauly, MQ XXXIV (1948) 371–403, XXXV (1949) 85–105 (cf. Pauly, "Benedetto Marcello's . . .").

652 Margnof, Horst-Tanu. "Zur hallischen Aufführungspraxis der Händel-Oper," Händel-Festspiele (1954) 23–26, (1955) 80–82.

652.01 Marguerre, K. "Forte und Piano bei Mozart," NZfM CXXVIII (1967) 153–60 (dynamics, esp. in the violin sonatas).

652.02 Marpurg, Friedrich Wilhelm. *Abhandlung von den Manieren.* MS in Deutsche Staatsbibliothek, Mus. MS theor. 553, [1754] (ornamentation).

653 ———. *Anleitung zum Clavierspielen.* Berlin: Haude & Spener, 1755 (incl. fingering, tempo, ornamentation).

654 ———. *Anleitung zur Musik überhaupt, und zur Singkunst besonders.* Berlin: Arnold Wever, 1763 (incl. vocal ornamentation).

655 [———]. *Des Critischen musicus an der Spree erster Band.* Berlin: Haude & Spener, [issued weekly from 4 March 1749 to 17 February 1750] (incl. appended table of ornaments).

656 ——. *Handbuch bey dem Generalbasse und der Composition* . . . , 3 vols. in one with Appendices. Berlin: G. A. Lange, 1755–62.

657 ——. *Historisch-Kritische Beyträge zur Aufnahme der Musik,* 5 vols. Berlin: G. A. Lange, 1754–62, 1778.

658 [——]. *Die Kunst das Clavier zu spielen,* 4th ed. Berlin: Haude & Spener, 1762.

659 ——. Prefaces to *Clavierstücke mit einem practischen Unterricht für Anfänger und Geübtere,* 3 vols. Berlin: Haude & Spener, 1762–63 (incl. *b. c.*).

660 Martienssen, Carl Adolf. "Bach-Konzerte mit Flügel oder Cembalo?" Festschrift BACH-PROBLEME 70–73 (piano vs. harpsichord).

661 Martinelli, Vincenzio. *Lettre famigliari e critiche.* London: G. Nourse, 1758 (opera singing).

661.01 Martini, Jean Paul Égide. *Mélopée Moderne ou l'art du chant.* . . . Paris: Cochet, Luthier et Mᵈ de Musique, [1792?] (ornamentation, cadences).

661.02 Marx, Adolf Bernhard. *Anleitung zum Vortrag Beethovenscher Klavierwerke.* Berlin: 1863. Trans. by F. L. Gwinner as *Introduction to the Interpretation of the Beethoven Piano Works.* Chicago: Clayton F. Summy Co., 1895 (incl. fingering, articulation, rhythm, ornamentation).

662 ——. "Einige Bemerkungen über Studium und Vortrag der Beethovenschen Klavierwerke," *Ludwig van Beethoven, Leben und Schaffen,* II. Leipzig: Schumann, 1902.

663 Marx, Herbert. "Die Technik des Spiels auf alten Tasteninstrumenten," unpublished Ph.D. diss., Breslau, 1928 (to 18th century).

664 Marx, Josef. "The Tone of the Baroque Oboe," GSJ IV (1951) 3–19 (incl. shape of reed, pitch).

664.01 Mason, Wilton. "The Architecture of St. Mark's Cathedral and the Venetian Polychoral Style: A Clarification," Festschrift HAYDON 163–78 (disposition of choirs, organ accompaniment).

665 Masson, Charles. *Nouveau traité des regles pour la composition de la musique* . . . , 4th ed., rev. and cor. Amsterdam: E. Roger, [1710?] (*b. c.*).

666 Matthaei, Karl. "Johann Sebastian Bachs Orgel," Bachgedenkschrift 118–49 (registration).

667 Matthes, René. "Generalbass-Probleme in der modernen Aufführungspraxis," SMZ XCVII (1957) 432–39.

668 ——. "Lebendige Aufführungspraxis; Eine Einführung für Sänger und Dirigenten in die Auskolorierung Händelscher Oratorien," SMZ XCIX (1959) 301–08 (ornamentation).

669 Mattheson, Johann. *A Complete Treatise of Thorough Bass.* . . . London: Printed for P. Hodgson, [17—].

670 ——. *Exemplarische Organisten-Probe im Artikel vom General-Bass.* Hamburg: Im Schiller- und Kissnerischen-buch-laden, 1719. 2nd ed.

as *Grosse General-Bass-Schule*. Hamburg: J. C. Kissnersbuchladen, 1731.

671 ——. . . . *Kleine General-Bass-Schule*. . . . Hamburg: J. C. Kissner, 1735.

672 ——. *Der vollkommene Capellmeister*. Hamburg: C. Herold, 1739. Fac. ed. by M. Reimann. Kassel: Bärenreiter, 1954. Partial trans. by H. Lenneberg as "Johann Mattheson on Affect and Rhetoric in Music," *Journal of Music Theory* II (1958) 47–84, 193–236.

673 Maxton, Willy. "Zur Aufführungspraxis Dietrich Buxtehudes," MuK IV (1932) 268–77 (no. of singers, instrumentalists).

673.01 Maynard, Judson D. "Heir Beginnis Countering," JAMS XX (1967) 182–96.

674 Mazzocchi, Domenico. Preface to *Madrigali a Cinque Voci (1638)*. VogelB I 436–37 (directions for vocal and/or instrumental performance).

674.01 McCabe, William H. "Music and Dance on a 17th-Century College Stage," MQ XXIV (1938) 313–22 (esp. make-up of consorts).

675 McIntyre, Ray. "On the Interpretation of Bach's Gigues," MQ LI (1965) 478–92 (rhythm, quotes Brossard, J. Walther).

675.01 McKinnon, James W. "Musical Instruments in Medieval Psalm Commentaries and Psalters," JAMS XXI (1968) 3–20 (iconography).

676 Melchert, Hermann. "Das Rezitativ der Kirchenkantaten J. S. Bachs," BJ XLV (1958) 5–83 (incl. rhythm, *b. c.*).

677 ——. "Zum Rezitativ bei Johann Sebastian Bach," MuK XXIX (1959) 185–93 (incl. phrasing).

677.01 Meline, Florant. *The Modern Flute Professor*. . . . New York: by the author, 1821 (comprehensive, Baroque).

677.02 Melkus, Eduard. "Über die Ausführung der Stricharten in Mozarts Werken," Mozart Jb (1967) 244–65 (esp. bowing).

678 ——. "Zur Frage des Bach-Bogens," Österr MZ XI (1956) 99–105 (violin technique).

678.01 Mellers, Wilfrid. "Couperin on the Harpsichord," MT CIX (1968) 1010–11.

679 ——. "Theory and Practice," *François Couperin and the French Classical Tradition*. London: Dobson, 1950 (incl. rhythm, ornamentation, phrasing, tempo, bowing).

680 Mendel, Arthur. "On the Keyboard Accompaniments to Bach's Leipzig Church Music," MQ XXXVI (1950) 339–62.

681 ——. "On the Pitches in Use in Bach's Time," MQ XLI (1955) 332–354, 466–80.

682 ——. Review of "Ornamentation in J. S. Bach's Organ Works," by Putnam Aldrich, MQ XXXVII (1951) 290–94.

683 ——. "Pitch in the 16th and Early 17th Centuries," MQ XXXIV (1948) 28–45, 199–221, 336–57, 575–93.

684 —— (ed.). Preface to J. S. Bach's *Passion According to St. John*. New York: G. Schirmer, 1951 (incl. make-up of group, rhythm, tempo, fermatas, ornamentation, recitatives, *b. c.*, dynamics).

685 —— (ed.). Preface to Heinrich Schütz' *Historia von der Geburt Jesu Christi*. New York: G. Schirmer, 1949 (incl. recitative, *b. c.*, instrumentation, tempo).

686 —— (ed.). Preface to Heinrich Schütz' *Musicalische Exquien*. New York: G. Schirmer, 1957 (incl. use of violone).

687 ——. "Traces of the Pre-History of Bach's St. John and St. Matthew Passions," *Festschrift Otto Erich Deutsch zum 80. Geburtstag am 5. September 1963*, ed. by W. Gerstenberg, J. LaRue und W. Rehm. Kassel: Bärenreiter, 1963 31–48 (orchestration).

688 Mersenne, Marin. *Harmonie universelle*, 2 vols. Paris: S. Cramoisy, 1636–37. The books on instruments trans. by R. E. Chapman. The Hague: M. Nijhoff, 1957 (esp. instruments).

689 Mersmann, Hans. "Beiträge zur Aufführungspraxis der vorklassischen Kammermusik in Deutschland," AfMw II (1920) 99–143 (ornamentation).

690 Mertin, Josef. "Aufführungspraxis alter Musik. Der historische A-cappella Begriff," Österr MZ XIII (1958) 362–65 (before 1600).

691 ——. "Die Aufführungspraxis alter Musik. Das Stimmengleichgewicht," Österr MZ XIV (1959) 57–62 (ensemble performance).

692 ——. "Die Aufführungspraxis alter Musik. Notation und Raumakustik," Österr MZ XIV (1959) 112–16.

693 ——. "Das Instrumentarium der alten Ensemblemusik. (III. Die Orgeln)," Österr MZ XIII (1958) 513–18.

694 ——. "Das Instrumentarium der alten Ensemblemusik (IV. Die saiteninstrumente)," Österr MZ XIV (1959) 11–17.

695 ——. "Das Instrumentarium der alten Musik. (Renaissance und Gotik) —Die Blaseninstrumente," Österr MZ XIII (1958) 409–15.

696 ——. "Metrum und Aufführungspraxis," Österr MZ XVI (1961) 513–18 (to Classic).

697 ——. Über Aufführungspraxis historischer Sakralmusik," *Bericht . . . zweiter Internationaler Kongress für Katholische Kirchenmusik Wien 4.–10. Oktober, 1954*. Vienna: 1955 188–92 (instrumental and choral make-up).

698 ——. "Über musikalische Ornamentik," Österr MZ XVII (1962) 114–24 (Baroque).

699 ——. "Zur Aufführungspraxis in der Musik von Heinrich Schütz," Österr MZ XXI (1966) 166–76.

699.01 ——. "Zur Verwendung der Singstimme in alter Musik," Österr MZ XXII (1967) 178–89 (incl. falsetto, scoring, pitch).

700 Metcalfe, William C. "Dolce or Traverso? The Flauto Problem in

Vivaldi's Instrumental Music," AR VI/3 (1965) 3–6 (flute vs. recorder).

701 ——. "The Recorder Cantatas of Telemann's *Harmonischer Gottesdienst*," AR VIII/4 (1967) 113–18 (incl. tempo, instrumentation, recitatives).

701.01 Meyer, Ernst Hermann. "Zur Frage der Aufführung alter Musik," *Festschrift für Walter Wiora zum 30. Dezember 1966*, ed. L. Finscher and C.-H. Mahling. Kassel: Bärenreiter, 1967 57–61.

702 Meyer, Ralph. "Die Behandlung des Rezitativs in Glucks italienischen Reformopern," Gluck Jb (1918) 1–90 (rhythm).

703 Meyer, Ramon E. "John Playford's *An Introduction to the Skill of Musick*," unpublished Ph.D. diss., Florida State University, 1961 (incl. singing, stringed instruments).

703.01 Mezger, Manfred. "Bachstil heute," MuK XXXVIII (1968) 209–21 (general).

704 Mies, Paul. "Die Artikulationszeichen Strich und Punkt bei Wolfgang Amadeus Mozart," Mf XI (1958) 428–55.

705 ——. "Die Entwürfe Franz Schuberts zu den letzten drei Klaviersonaten von 1828," BzMw II (1960) 52–68 (incl. rhythm).

706 ——. "Über ein besonderes Akzentzeichen bei Johannes Brahms," BzMw V (1963) 213–22 (rhythmic accent).

707 ——. "Über ein besonderes Akzentzeichen bei Joh. Brahms," KONGRESS 1962 (Kassel) 215–17 (articulation, dynamics).

708 Miller, Edward. *Elements of Thorough Bass and Composition . . . Opera Quinta*. London: Longman & Broderip [1787], and Dublin: E. Lee, [1787].

709 Miller, James Earl. "The Life and Works of Jan Václav Stich (Giovanni Punto)," unpublished Ph.D. diss., State University of Iowa, 1962 (incl. instrumental technique).

710 Mizler [von Kolof], Lorenz [Christoph]. *Anfangs-Gründe des General Basses*. . . . Leipzig: zu finden bey dem Verfasser, [1739] (cf. Andrieu, *Kurtze* . . .).

711 ——. *Musikalischer Staarstecher*. . . . Leipzig: Auf kosten des Verfassers, [1740] (singing).

711.01 Moldenhauer, Hans. "A Newly Found Mozart Autograph: Two Cadenzas to K. 107," JAMS VIII (1955) 213–16.

712 Monici, A. "Delle regole più essenziali per imparare a cantare; secondo un vecchio autore," RMI XVIII (1911) 85–94 (discusses Vincenzo Manfredini's "Regole Armoniche . . .," ornamentation, improvisation).

713 Montéclair, Michel Pignolet de. *Méthode facile pour apprendre à jouer du violon*, Paris: 1712.

713.01 ——. *Nouvelle Méthode pour apprendre la Musique*. . . . Paris: l'auteur, 1709 (incl. ornamentation).

713.02 ——. *Principes de musique divisez en quatre parties.* Paris: [Boivin, 1739] (incl. ornamentation).

714 Monteverdi, Claudio. Preface to *Madrigali Guerrieri et Amorosi (1638),* VogelB I 511–13 (incl. *b. c.*).

715 Monteverdi, Guilio Cesare. Preface to Claudio Monteverdi's *Scherzi Musicali a tre Voci . . . 1607,* VogelB I 515–16 (text/music relationship).

715.01 Moraes Pedroso, Manoel de. *Compendio Musico, ou arte abbreviada em que se contèm as regras mais necessarias da cantoria, acompanhamento, e contraponto. . . .* Porto: Na Officina de Antonio Alvares Riveiro Guimaraens, 1769.

716 Morley, Thomas. *A Plaine and Easie Introduction to Practicall Musick.* London: P. Short, 1597. Fac. ed. by E. H. Fellowes. London: Shakespeare Assoc., 1937. Ed. by R. Harman. London: Dent, 1952.

717 Moscheles, Ignace. "Musical Observations" *The Life of Beethoven,* II. London: Colburn, 1841 (incl. tempo, Beethoven's playing).

718 Moser, Andreas. *Geschichte des Violinspiels,* 2nd ed., rev. by H. J. Nösselt, with introduction by H. J. Moser, I. Tutzing: Hans Schneider, 1966 (Italy).

719 ——. "Die Violin-Skordatur," AfMw I (1919) 573–89.

720 ——. "Zur Frage der Ornamentik und ihrer Anwendung auf Corellis Op. 5," ZfMw I (1918–19) 287–93.

721 Moser, Hans Joachim. *Heinrich Schütz: Sein Leben und Werk.* Kassel: Bärenreiter-Verlag, 1954. Trans. by C. F. Pflattleicher as *Heinrich Schütz: His Life and Work.* St. Louis: Concordia, 1959 (incl. instrumentation, tempo, etc.).

722 ——. "Instrumentalismen bei Ludwig Senfl," Festschrift WOLF 123–138.

723 ——. "Nochmals die Fermatenfrage," MuK III (1931) 72–75.

723.01 —— (ed.). Preface to Johann Kuhnau's *Klavierwerke.* DDT IV (ornamentation).

724 ——. "Seb. Bachs Stellung zur Choralrhythmik der Lutherzeit," BJ XIV (1917) 57–79.

725 ——. "Zum Fermatenproblem," MuK II (1930) 257–61 (cf. *supra*).

726 ——. "Zur Ausführung der Ornamente bei Bach," *Musik in Zeit und Raum,* ausgewählte Abhandlungen. Berlin: Merseburger, 1960 159–72.

727 ——. "Zur Frage der Ausführung der Ornamente bei Bach," BJ XIII (1916) 8–19 (cf. *supra*).

728 Mozart, J. C. Wolfgang Amadeus. *Kurzgefasste Generalbass-Schule.* Vienna: S. A. Steiner und Comp., [1818]. Subsequently published as *Fundament des General-Basses.* Berlin: In der Schüppelschen Buchlandlung, 1822. Trans. by S. G. Gödbe as *Mozart's Practical Elements of Thorough Bass. . . .* London: R. Cocks &

Co., [n. d.] (considered spurious: cf. Köchel Catalogue, 6th ed., Anhang C30.04).

729 ——. *The Letters of Mozart and his Family*, trans. and ed. by E. Anderson, 3 vols. London: Macmillan and Co., Ltd., 1938.

730 Mozart, J. G. Leopold. *Versuch einer gründlichen Violinschule.* Augsburg: J. J. Lotter, 1756. [Fac. of 1st ed.], ed. by B. Paumgartner. Vienna: C. Stephenson, [1922]. Trans. by E. Knocker as *A Treatise on the Fundamental Principles of Violin Playing.* London: Oxford University Press, 1948.

731 Müller, August Eberhard. *Anweisung zum genauen Vortrage der Mozartschen Clavierconcerte hauptsichlich in Absicht richtiger Applicatur.* Leipzig: Breitkopf & Härtel, 1796 (incl. fingering).

732 ——. *Elementarbuch für Flötenspieler. . . .* Leipzig: C. F. Peters, 1815.

733 ——. *Grosse Fortepiano-Schule*, 8th ed. by C. Czerny. Leipzig: C. F. Peters, [18—] (incl. fingering, ornaments, tuning, *b. c.*).

734 ——. *Klavier- und Fortepiano-Schule . . .*, ed. by G. S. Löhein. Jena: Friedrich Frommann, 1804 (incl. fingering, ornaments, tempo, *b. c.*).

735 Müller, Fritz. "Darf man zu Bachs Kirchenmusik das Cembalo verwenden?" MuK VIII (1936) 79–80 (organ vs. harpsichord) (cf. Jansen, "Cembalo . . .").

736 Müller, Hermann. "Der Musiktraktat in dem Werke des Bartholomaeus Anglicus De proprietatibus rerum," Festschrift RIEMANN 241–55 (incl. singing, instruments).

737 Müller, Karl Friedrich. "Die Technik der Ausdrucksdarstellung in Monteverdis monodischen Frühwerken," unpublished Ph.D. diss., Berlin, 1931.

738 Müller, Theodor. "Grundsätzliches zur Interpretation der Violinwerke W. A. Mozarts," Festschrift PAUMGARTNER 119–27 (musical symbols).

739 Müller, Werner. "Das Ausdrucksproblem in der Klaviermusik C. Ph. E. Bachs," unpublished Ph.D. diss., Saarbrücken, 1959.

740 Müller-Blattau, Joseph. "Bindung und Freiheit; Zu W. Fr. Bachs Fugen und Polonaisen," *Festschrift Wilhelm Fischer zum 70. Geburtstag überreicht im Mozartjahr 1956 . . .*, ed. by H. Zingerle. Innsbruck: Sprachwissenschaftliches Seminar der Univ. Innsbruck, 1956 83–98 (esp. dynamics).

740.01 —— (ed.). *Die Kompositionslehre Heinrich Schützens in der Fassung seines Schülers Christoph Bernhard.* Leipzig: Breitkopf & Härtel, 1926 (esp. Part B, incl. diminution).

741 ——. "Zur vokalen Improvisation im 16. Jahrhundert," KONGRESS 1958 (Cologne) 195–96.

742 Münster, Robert. "Authentische Tempi zu den sechs letzten Sinfonien W. A. Mozarts?" Mozart Jb (1962–63) 185–99.

71

742.01 Muffat, Georg. Preface to *Apparatus musico-organisticus, Liber Primus.* Salzburg: Joan. Bapt. Mayr, 1690 (ornamentation).

743 ——. Preface to *Ausserlesene . . . Instrumental-Music (1701),* DTÖ XXIII (incl. dynamics, tempo, make-up of group).

744 ——. Preface to *Florilegium Primum für Streichinstrumente . . .,* DTÖ II (*notes inégales,* tempo, repetition).

745 ——. Preface to *Florilegium Secundum für Streichinstrumente . . .,* DTÖ IV (ornamentation, tempo, bowing) (cf. Cooper and Zsako, "George Muffatt's . . .").

746 ——. Preface to *Sechs Concerti Grossi I* DTÖ XXIII (instruments for *b. c.,* dynamics).

747 ——. "Regulae concentuum partiturae . . .," MS Vienna Minoritenkonvent, 1699; trans. by H. Federhofer as *An Essay on Thoroughbass.* [Rome]: American Institute of Musicology, 1961.

747.01 Muffat, Gottlieb. From *Componimenti Musicali per il Cembalo.* . . . Augsburg: Christian Leopold, [173–]. Ed. by F. Chrysander in DTÖ VII as *Supplemente, enthaltend Quellen zu Händel's Werken, Vol. V* (incl. table of ornaments).

748 ——. Preface to *Sept Suites pour le Clavecin, Le Trésor des Pianistes* VII (incl. table of ornaments).

749 ——. Preface to *Zwölf Toccaten und 72 Versetl für Orgel und Klavier,* DTÖ LVIII (ornaments).

749.01 Murphy, Sylvia. "Seventeenth-Century Guitar Music: Notes on *Rasgueado* Performance," GSJ XXI (1968) 24–32 (right-hand techniques).

750 Murray, Sidney. "Jean-Antoine Bérard's *L'art du chant:* A Translation and Commentary," unpublished Ph.D. diss., State University of Iowa, 1955.

751 *The Muses' Delight.* Liverpool: John Sadler, 1754 (ornamentation, improvisation).

752 Mylius, Wolfgang Michael. *Rudimenta musices . . . Anweisung zur Singekunst.* Gotha: in Verlegung des Autoris, 1686 (incl. ornamentation).

N

753 Nagel, Wilibald. "John Douland's Necessarie Observations belonging to Lute-playing," MfM XXIII (1891) 145–62 (German trans. of and commentary on Robert Dowland's *Varietie of Lute-Lessons . . .* [1610]) (cf. **271.002**).

753.001 Nares, [James]. *A Concise and Easy Treatise on Singing, Addressed to the Dilettanti in Music, . . .* London: for the Author, [178–?] (incl. diminutions).

753.01 Nassarre, Pablo. *Escvela musica, segun la practica moderna,* 2 vols. Saragossa: Larumbe, 1724 (incl. *glossas*).

754 Nathan, Hans. "The Sense of History in Musical Interpretation," MR XIII (1952) 85–100 (incl. tempo, timbre).

755 Nathan, Isaac. *Musurgia Vocalis* . . . , 2nd ed. London: Fentum, 1836. Ed. E. Foreman in *The Porpora Tradition*, Champaign: Pro Musica Press, 1968 (cf. Corri, *Singer's* . . .).

756 Nauss, Johan Xaver. *Gründlicher Unterricht den General-Bass recht zu erlernen* . . . , 2nd ed. Augsburg: J. J. Lotter, 1769.

757 Neemann, Hans. "Laute und Theorbe als Generalbassinstrumente im 17. und 18. Jahrhundert," Zf Mw XVI (1934) 527–34.

758 ——. "Spieltechnik," *Lautenmusik des 17./18. Jahrhunderts*, EdM XII (quotes Reusner's *Neue Lauten Früchte* [1676] on hand placements and fingering).

759 Nef, Karl. "Clavicymbel und Clavichord," JbP X (1903) 15–30 (clavichord vs. harpsichord).

760 ——. "Zur Instrumentation im 17. Jahrhundert," JbP XXXV (1928) 33–42.

761 Neufeldt, Ernst. "Zur Frage der Aufführung alter Musik," Mk XI/2 (1911–12) 278–83.

761.01 Neumann, Frederick. "External Evidence and Uneven Notes," MQ LII (1966) 448–64 (esp. J. S. Bach).

762 ——. "The French Inégales, Quantz, and Bach," JAMS XVIII (1965) 313–58.

763 ——. "Misconceptions about the French Trill in the 17th and 18th Centuries," MQ L (1964) 188–206 (implications for Bach).

764 ——. "A New Look at Bach's Ornamentation," ML XLVI (1965) 4–15, 126–33.

765 ——. "La note pointée at la soi-disant 'manière française,'" RM1 LI (1965) 66–92 (dotted notes and *notes inégales*).

765.01 ——. "Notes on 'Melodic' and 'Harmonic' Ornaments," MR XXIX (1968) 249–56.

766 ——. "The Use of Baroque Treatises on Musical Performance," ML XLVIII (1967) 315–24.

766.01 Neumann, Werner. "Probleme der Aufführungspraxis im Spiegel der Geschichte der Neuen Bachgesellschaft," BJ (1967) 100–20 (organ, keyboard, vocal works).

767 Neumann, Werner. "Zur Aufführungspraxis der Kantate 152," BJ XXXVIII (1949–50) 100–03 (incl. instrumentation, transposition).

768 Neumayr, Heinrich. "Musik auf alten Werken der bildenden Kunst," Österr MZ XV (1960) 553–59 (iconography).

769 Neupert, Hanns. *The Clavichord*, trans. from the German by A. P. P. Feldberg. Kassel: Bärenreiter, 1965 (Baroque).

769.01 *New and Complete Pocket Preceptor for the English & French Flagelets.* . . . London: George Astor, [179–?] (comprehensive).

769.02 *The Newest Method for Learners on the German Flute.* . . . London: Printing Office, [1731] (graces, articulation).

770 Newman, Joel. "Some Ornaments in Renaissance Ensemble Music," AR VII/4 (1966) 10–11 (quotes Vecchi, Rossi, Staden).

771 Newman, William S. "Concerning the Accompanied Clavier Sonata," MQ XXXIII (1947) 327–49 (texture).

771.01 ——. "Is There a Rationale for the Articulation of J. S. Bach's String and Wind Music?" Festschrift HAYDON 229–44.

772 ——. "Styles and Touches in Bach's Keyboard Music," (Summy Piano Teaching Pamphlet Ser. 8.) Chicago: Summy Publications, 1956.

773 [Newton, Sir Isaac]. "Out of Mr. Sympsons Division violist," Cambridge University Library MS (Add. 3970), [n. d.] (*b. c.*).

774 Nicholson, James. *A Concise Treatise on Thorough Bass.* . . . London: Bland & Weller's Music Warehouse, [1796?] (incl. realizations).

775 Niecks, Frederick. "An Old Reading or Supposed Old Reading of Dotted Notes," MMR XLII (1912) 197–99 (quotes Leopold Mozart and Quantz).

775.01 ——. "On the Use and Abuse of the Pedal," MMR VI (1876) 179–83 (19th century).

776 ——. "Tempo Rubato," MMR XLIII (1913) 29–31, 58–59.

777 Niedt, Friedrich Erhard. *Musicalische Handleitung . . . Erster Theil.* Hamburg: B. Schillern, 1700. 2nd pt. as *Handleitung zur Variation.* Hamburg: auf kosten des autoris, und bey B. Schillern zu finden, 1706. *Musicalischer Handleitung dritter und letzter Theil.* Hamburg: 1717 (inc. *b. c.*).

777.001 Nivers, Guillaume Gabriel. Preface to *Livre d'orgue.* . . . 3 vols. Paris: C. Ballard, 1665–67 (incl. ornamentation, registration).

777.01 Nolte, Ewald V. "The Magnificat Fugues of Johann Pachelbel: Alternation or Intonation?" JAMS IX (1956) 19–24.

777.02 Norden, N. Lindsay. "A New Theory of Untempered Music," MQ XXII (1936) 217–33 (a cappella music).

778 Norlind, Tobias. "Die Schwedische Hofkapelle in der Reformationszeit," Festschrift WOLF 148–52 (instruments used).

779 North, Roger. *Memoirs of Musick*, ed. and ann. by E. F. Rimbault. London: G. Bell, 1846 (17th and 18th centuries).

780 Nottebohm, Gustav. *Beethoveniana, Aufsätze und Mittheilungen.* Leipzig & Winterthur: J. Rieter-Biedermann, 1872 (incl. dynamics, articulation, metronomic markings, etc.).

O

780.01 Oberborbeck, Felix. "'Vor deinen Thron tret ich hiemit.' Bemerkungen zu Geschichte, Form und Aufführungspraxis von Bachs

Lebensepilog," *Bericht über die Wissenschaftliche Bachtagung.*
Leipzig: C. F. Peters 1951 285–93.

781 Oberdörffer, Fritz. "Generalbass," MGG IV Col. 1708–37 (incl.
bibliography).

782 ——. *Der Generalbass in der Instrumentalmusik des ausgehenden 18. Jahrhunderts.* Kassel: Bärenreiter-Verlag, 1939.

783 ——. "Neuere Generalbassstudien," AMl XXXIX (1967) 182–201.

784 ——. "Über die Generalbassbegleitung zu Kammermusikwerken
Bachs; Schlusswort," Mf XI (1958) 79–82 (cf. **783, 785,** and
994).

785 ——. "Über die Generalbassbegleitung zu Kammermusikwerken
Bachs und des Spätbarock," Mf X (1957) 61–74 (cf. **783, 784,**
and **994**).

786 Ochs, Siegfried. "Werke von Georg Friedrich Handel," *Der deutsche
Gesangverein,* II. Berlin: M. Hesse, 1924 52–128.

787 Orff, Carl. "Neugestaltung des *Orfeo* von Claudio Monteverdi," SMZ
LXXI (1931) 169–77 (instrumentation, *b. c.,* trans. in Orff's
edition of *Orfeo*).

787.01 Ornithoparcus, Andreas. *Musice Actiue Microlog.* . . . Leipzig: 1517.
Trans. by J. Dowland as *Andreas Ornithoparcus. His Micrologvs of
Introduction: Containing the Art of Singing.* . . . London: Thomas
Adams, 1609 (incl. rhythm, tempo, *musica ficta*).

788 Ortiz, Diego. *Tratado de glosas sobre clausulas y otros generos de puntos en
la musica de violones.* Rome: Valerio Dorico, 1553 (incl. ornamentation, improvisation).

788.01 Osthoff, Wolfgang. "Claudio Monteverdi in Unserer Zeit," *Musica*
XXI (1967) 203–16 (expression).

789 Ottich, Maria. *Die Bedeutung des Ornaments im Schaffen Friedrich Chopins.*
Berlin: Funk (1937).

790 Ozi, [Étienne]. *Méthode Nouvelle et Raisonnée pour le Basson* [1787].
Paris: Naderman, [180–] (incl. doubling, ornaments, etc.).

P

790.01 Paccagnella, Ermenegildo. *Abbellimenti musicali,* 3rd ed. Monza:
Arti Grafiche Monza, 1925 (most examples illustrate Bach or
Beethoven, although other composers, such as Purcell, Rameau,
Schumann, and Chopin, are represented).

790.02 Paesler, Carl. "Fundamentbuch von Hans von Constanz," VfMw
V (1889) 1–192 (incl. ornamentation).

791 —— (ed.). Preface to Johann Kuhnau's *Klavierwerke,* DDT IV
(ornaments).

792 Paisiello, Giovanni. *Regole per bene accompagnare il Partimento, o sia il
Basso Fondamentale Sopra il cembalo.* St. Petersburg: 1782.

792.001 Paixão Ribeiro, Manoel da. *Nova arte de viola.* . . . Coimbra: Fra Real
Officina da Universidade, 1789 (incl. tuning, accompaniment).

792.002 Palisca, Claude V. "The First Performance of 'Euridice,'" *Twenty-Fifth Anniversary Festschrift (1939–1962)*, ed. by A. Mell. New York: Queens College Press, 1964, 1–24 (circumstances, forces).

792.01 ——. "Vincenzo Galilei's Counterpoint Treatise: A Code for the *Seconda Practica*," JAMS IX (1956) 81–96 (monody, (*b. c.*).

793 Parrish, Carl. "The Early Piano and its Influence on Keyboard Technique and Composition in the Eighteenth Century," unpublished Ph.D. diss., Harvard University, 1939. Superior: Research Microfilm Publishers, 1953.

793.01 ——. "Haydn and the Piano," JAMS I/3 (1948) 27–34 (harpsichord vs. piano).

794 Pasquali, Nicolo. *The Art of Fingering the Harpsichord.* . . . Edinburgh: R. Bremner, [1760?] (incl. ornaments, tuning).

795 ——. *Thorough-Bass Made Easy.* . . . London: Robt. Bremner, [17—]. Edinburg: Robt. Bremner, [1757]. London: Broderip & Wilkinson, [180–].

796 [Pauer, Ernst]. "The 'Agréments' of Rameau and Couperin," MMR IV (1874) 64–66.

796.01 Paul, James Ector. "Vitalizing Elements in the Performance of Baroque Choral and Instrumental Music as Revealed in the Study of Performance Practice (with) Full Scores of Two Baroque Choral Compositions," unpublished D.M.A. diss., University of Washington, 1966 (discussion of Monteverdi's *Lagrime d'Amante al Sepolcro dell'Amate* and Handel's Chandos Anthem *O Come, Let us Sing*; tempo, expression, ornamentation).

797 Pauly, Reinhard G. "Benedetto Marcello's Satire on Early 18th-Century Opera," MQ XXXIV (1948) 222–33 (cf. Marcello, "Il Teatro . . .").

797.01 Paumann, Conrad. *Fundamentum organisandi.* 1453. Fac. ed. by Ameln. Kassel: Bärenreiter, [n. d.] (fac. ed. incl. Locheimer Liederbuch, diminution).

797.02 Penna, Lorenzo. *Li Primi Albori per li Principianti della Musica figurata.* Bologna: Giacomo Monti, 1672 (*b. c.*).

798 Peri, Jacopo. Preface to *L'Euridice (1600)*. VogelB II 64–66 (monody).

798.01 Perkins, Marian Louise. "Changing Concepts of Rhythm in the Romantic Era. A Study of Rhythmic Structure, Theory, and Performance Practices Related to Piano Literature," unpublished Ph.D. diss., University of Southern California, 1961 (tempo rubato, dynamics, phrasing).

799 Pessl, Yella. "French Patterns and Their Reading in Bach's Secular Clavier Music," AMS Papers (1941) 8–20 (ornamentation, *notes inégales*).

800 Peterson, Franklin. "Alla Breve," MMR XXVII (1897) 147–50 (18th and 19th centuries).

801 ——. "The Registration of Bach's Organ Works," MMR XXVIII (1898) 97–99 (incl. dynamics).

802 Petri, Johann Samuel. *Anleitung zur practischen Musik, vor neuangehende Sänger und Instrumentspieler.* Lauban: J. C. Wirthgen, 1767.

803 Pfannkuch, Wilhelm. "J. S. Bachs 'Musikalisches Opfer,'" Mf VII (1954) 440–53 (instrumentation and arrangement).

804 Pfrogner, Hermann. "Der Clavis in Andreas Werckmeisters 'Nothwendigsten Anmerkungen und Regeln' wie der Bassus continuus oder Generalbass wol könne tractiret werden," KONGRESS 1953 (Bamberg) 149–51.

804.01 Pierce, Edwin Hall. "The Significance of the 'Trill,' as Found in Beethoven's Most Mature Works," MQ XV (1929) 233–45.

804.02 Pincherle, Marc. "De l'ornamentation des sonates de Corelli," *Feuillets d'histoire du violon.* Paris: G. Legouix, 1927.

805 ——. "Elementary Musical Instruction in the 18th Century," MQ XXXIV (1948) 61—67 (singing).

806 ——. "L'Exécution aux XVIIᵉ et XVIIIᵉ siècles: Instruments à archet," KONGRESS 1961 (New York) 220–31.

806.01 ——. "Florid Ornamentation," *The Consort* No. 7 (1950) 21–25 (quotes *Corelli's Solos, grac'd by Doburg*).

807 ——. "L'Interpretazione orchestrale di Lulli," Festschrift MARINUZZI 139–52.

808 ——. "On the Rights of the Interpreter in the Performance of 17th- and 18th-Century Music," MQ XLIV (1958) 145–66 (form, sonority, bowing, rhythm, harmony, ornamentation).

809 —— (ed.). Preface to Jean Joseph Cassanea de Mondonville's *Pièces de clavecin en sonates*, PSFM, Ser. I, Vol. IX (violin accompaniment and ornamentation).

810 ——. "Sur une cadence-caprice pour violon de l'an 1695," RM1 III (1922) 164–67 (realized cadenza).

811 Pirro, André. "Comment jouer Bach sur l'orgue," RM (1932) 356–62 (esp. chorale preludes).

812 ——. "Les 'Frottole' et la musique instrumentale," RM1 III (1922) 3–12.

812.01 —— (ed.). Preface to Jacques Boyvin's *Oeuvres complètes d'Orgue.* Mayence-Leipzig: B. Schott's Söhne, [1905] (ornamentation).

813 ——. "Remarques sur l'exécution musicale, de la fin du 14ᵉ au milieu du 15ᵉ siècle," KONGRESS 1930 (Liège) 55–65.

814 Platen, Emil. "Zur Frage den Kürzungen in der Dacapoformen J. S. Bachs," Festschrift SCHMIDT-GÖRG (60) 224–34.

815 Playford, John. *A Breefe Introduction to the Skill of Musick for Song and Violl*, at least 19 and several more unnumbered eds. London: [various publishers], 1655–1730 (cf. Meyer, Ramon, "John Playford's . . .") (incl. singing, viol).

77

816 Pleyel, Ignaz. *Klavierschule*, 3rd ed. Leipzig: Hoffmeister & Kühnel, 1804 (incl. ornaments, fingering, tempo).

816.001 Pochon, Alfred. *Le Rôle du point en musique.* . . . Lausanne: Librairie F. Rouge & Cie, 1947.

816.01 Polk, Keith. "Flemish Wind Bands in the Late Middle Ages, A Study in Improvisatory Performance Practices," unpublished Ph.D. diss., University of California at Berkeley, 1968.

817 Pollini, Francesco. *Metodo pel clavicembalo*, 2nd ed. Milan: G. Ricordi, [183–].

817.01 Porter, Ernest. "Schubert's Appoggiaturas: A Further Note," MT CIV (1963) 110–11.

818 Portmann, Johann Gottlieb. *Leichtes Lehrbuch der Harmonie, Composition und des Generalbasses.* . . . Darmstadt: J. J. Will, 1789.

819 Powell, Newman Wilson. "Rhythmic Freedom in the Performance of French Music from 1650 to 1735," unpublished Ph.D. diss., Stanford University, 1958 (incl. rhythm, *notes inégales*, tempo, ornaments).

820 Praetorius, Michael. *Syntagma musicum*, 3 vols. Wittenberg and Wolfenbüttel: [n. p.], 1615–20. Fac. ed. W. Gurlitt, 3 vols. Kassel: Bärenreiter, 1958–59 (incl. singing, instruments).

821 Preindl, Joseph. *Wiener-Tonschule* . . . , ed. by I. R. von Seyfried. Vienna: Tobias Haslinger, [1827] (*b. c.*).

822 [Prelleur, Peter]. *An Introduction to Singing After so Easy a Method.* . . . London: D. Rutherford, [17—] (incl. *b. c.*).

822.01 [———.]. *The Modern Musick Master or The Universal Musician.* London Printing Office in Bow Church, 1730. (cf. **436**).

823 [———]. *The Modern Musick-Master*, 4th ed. London: At the Printing-office in Bow Church Yard, 1731. Fac. ed. by A. H. King. Kassel: Bärenreiter, 1965 (incl. flute, oboe, violin, harpsichord).

823.01 Preston, Robert E. (ed.). Preface to Jean-Marie Leclair's *Sonatas for Violin and Basso Continuo, Op. 5, I–V*. New Haven: A–R Editions, 1968 (*b. c.*, ornamentation, bowing).

823.02 ———. "The Sonatas for Violin and Figured Bass by Jean-Marie Leclair L'Aîné," unpublished Ph.D. diss., University of Michigan, 1959 (second section incl. ornamentation).

824 Pringsheim, Heinz. "Vorhalt und Vorschlag," *Das Musikleben* VI (1953) 49–52.

824.01 Printz, Wolfgang Caspar. *Compendium musicae Signatoriae & Modulatoriae vocalis,* . . . Dresden and Leipzig: bey Johann Christoph Miethen, 1714 (rhythm, ornamentation; incl. list of instruments used with vocal music).

824.02 ———. . . . *Phrynis oder Satyrischer Componist.* . . . Quedlingburg: Christian Okel, 1676–77 (esp. ornamentation, *b. c.*).

825 [Prixner, Sebastian]. *Kann man nicht in zwey, oder drey Monaten die*

Orgel gut, und regelmässig schlagen lernen? . . . Landshut: Mit Hagenschen schriften, 1789 (incl. *b. c.*).

826 Prod'homme, Jacques-Gabriel. "Notes d'archives concernant l'emploi des clarinettes en 1763," RM1 (1919) 192–94.

826.01 Prout, Ebenezer. "The Orchestra in 1800 and in 1900," MMR XXVI (1896) 25–31 (incl. Beethoven, Weber, Schubert, Mendelssohn, Brahms).

827 —— (ed.). Preface to Johann Sebastian Bach's *Piano Compositions*, II. Boston: O. Ditson, 1908 (rhythm, ornamentation, phrasing).

827.01 ——. "The Proper Balance of Chorus and Orchestra," MMR XXXI (1901) 26–27, 51–53 (19th century).

828 ——. "Some Musical Conventions of the Eighteenth Century," MMR XXXIX (1909) 265–68 (rhythm, ornaments, key-signatures).

829 Prunières, Henry. "De l'interprétation des agréments du chant aux XVIIᵉ et XVIIIᵉ siècles," RM (May, 1932) 329–44.

830 ——. "*L'Orfeo* de Monteverdi," RM (August, 1923) 20–34 (diminution).

831 Pujol, Emilio. "Significación de Joan Carlos Amat (1572–1642) en la historia de la guitarra," AnM V (1950) 125–46 (discusses Amat's "Guitarra Española . . ." and other writings).

832 Purcell, Henry. Preface to *A Choice Collection of Lessons for the Harpsichord or Spinnet*, 3rd ed. London: 1699 (incl. tempo, ornaments).

833 ——. Preface to *Complete Works*, Vol. VI, ed. by W. Barclay Squire and E. J. Hopkins. London: Novello, 1895 (tempo, ornaments, fingering).

Q

834 [Quantz, Johann Joachim]. "Discours des Herrn Quanz über das Clavier-accompagnement, (1763)," MfM XVI (1884) 120–22, 127–29 (*b. c.*, embellishment).

835 ——. *Versuch einer Anweisung die Flöte traversiere zu spielen.* . . . Berlin: Johann Friedrich Voss, 1752. Fac. of 3rd ed. (1789), ed. by H.-P. Schmitz. Kassel: Bärenreiter, 1953; trans. and ed. by E. R. Reilly as *On Playing the Flute.* New York: Free Press, 1966.

836 Quitin, José. "Les compositions de musique religieuse d'André-Modeste Grétry," RB XVIII (1964) 57–69 (instrumentation).

R

837 Raček, Jan. "Les Madrigaux à voix seule de Luzzasco Luzzaschi," RM (June 1932) 11–23 (diminution).

838 Raeburn, Christopher "Das Zeitmass in Mozarts Opern," Österr MZ XII (1957) 329–33.

839 Raguenet, l'abbé François. *Parallele des Italiens et des François, en ce* *qui regarde la musique et les opéra*. Paris: Jean Moreau, 1602 [i.e. 1702]. Trans. [attributed to J. E. Galliard by Sir John Hawkins] as *A Comparison between the French and Italian Musick and Opera's*. London: William Lewis, 1709. Galliard's trans. ed. by O. Strunk as "A Comparison Between the French and Italian Music," MQ XXXII (1946) 411–36 (French vs. Italian opera; Eng. trans. incl. annotations on Eng. opera) (cf. Le Cerf, *Comparison* . . .).

840 Rameau, Jean-Philippe. *Code de musique pratique, ou méthodes pour apprendre la musique*. . . . Paris: L'Imprimerie Royale, 1760 (*b. c.*).

841 ——. *Dissertation sur les differentes méthodes d'accompagnement pour le clavecin, ou pour l'orgue*. Paris: [1732] (*b. c.*).

842 ——. Preface to *Pièces de clavecin*. [Paris: 1,706, 1724, 1731, c. 1728, 1741, 1747]. Ed. by E. R. Jacobi. Kassel: Bärenreiter, 1958.

843 Ramin, Günther. "Das Cembalo und seine kirchenmusikalische Verwendung," MuK VIII (1936) 216–19 (harpsichord vs. organ).

844 ——. "Die Improvisation im gottesdienstlichen Orgelspiel," MuK IV (1932) 158–61 (Baroque).

845 ——. "Zum Aufsatz 'Grundlagen der Orgeltechnik,'" MuK VI (1934) 127–30 (phrasing, articulation, fingering).

845.01 Ramsbotham, Alexander. "On Psalm-Chanting," ML I (1920) 208–17 (16th-century Anglican Chant).

845.02 Raparlier. *Principes de musique, les agréments du chant, et un essai sur la prononciation, l'articulation et la prosodie de la langue française*. Lille: chez P. S. Lalau, 1772 (ornaments, pronunciation, articulation).

846 Rasmussen, Mary. "On the Modern Performance of Parts Originally Written for the Cornett," BQ I (1957–58) 20–28 (articulation, timbre).

846.01 ——. "Some Notes on the Articulations in the Melodic Variation Tables of Johann Joachim Quantz's *Versuch* . . .," *Brass and Woodwind Quarterly* I (1966–67) 3–26.

847 Reaney, Gilbert. "The Performance of Medieval Music," Festschrift REESE 704–22 (use of instruments).

848 ——. "Voices and Instruments in the Music of Guillaume de Machaut," KONGRESS 1953 (Bamberg) 245–48.

849 ——. "Voices and Instruments in the Music of Guillaume de Machaut," RB X (1956) 3–17, 93–104.

850 Reddick, Harvey Phillips. "Johann Mattheson's Forty-Eight Thorough-Bass Test-Pieces: Translation and Commentary," unpublished Ph.D. diss., University of Michigan, 1956 (incl. realizations).

851 Redlich, Hans Ferdinand. "Claudio Monteverdi: Some Problems of Textual Interpretation," MQ XLI (1955) 66–75 (*b. c.*).

852 ——. "The Problems of Editing and Performance," *Claudio Monteverdi: Life and Works*, trans. by K. Dale. London: Oxford University Press 1952, 151–65 (esp. *1610 Vespers, Orfeo, Incoronazione di Poppea*).

853 Reese, Gustave. "The Repertoire of Book II of Ortiz's *Tratado*," *The Commonwealth of Music*, ed. by G. Reese and R. Brandel in Honor of Curt Sachs. New York: The Free Press, 1965. 201–07 (variations and ornamentation).

854 Refardt, Edgar. "Die Musik der Basler Volksschauspiele des 16. Jahrhunderts," *Musik in der Schweiz: Ausgewählte Aufsätze*. Bern: Verlag Paul Haupt, 1952 9–23 (instruments used for festivals).

855 ——. "Studien über den Rhythmus und seine Bedeutung," *Bulletin de la Société "Union musicologique"* III (1923) 18–44 (Haydn, Mozart, Beethoven).

856 Reichardt, Johann Friedrich. *Briefe eines aufmerksamen Reisenden die Musik betreffend*, 2 pts. Frankfurt and Leipzig: [n. p.], 1774–76.

857 Reinhard, Kurt. "Zur Frage des Tempos bei Chopin," KONGRESS 1960 (Chopin) 449–54.

858 Reinhard, Leonhard. *Kurzer und deutlicher Unterricht von dem General-Bass . . .*, [2nd ed.]. Augsburg: J. J. Lotters seel. erben, 1750.

859 Reinhart, Walther. *Die Aufführung der Johannes-Passion von J. S. Bach und deren Probleme*. Leipzig: Verlag Carl Merseburger, [c. 1933].

860 ——. "Einige Gedanken zur Praxis der Aufführung Bachscher Chorwerke mit Orchester, im besonderen der Kantaten," Bachgedenkschrift 84–102 (incl. make-up of group, dynamics, articulation, *b. c.*).

860.01 Rellstab, Johann Carl Friedrich. *C. P. E. Bach's Anfangstücke mit einer Anleitung für Clavierspieler, den Gebrauch der Bach'schen Fingersetzung, die Manieren und den Vortrag betreffend*. Berlin: [the author], 1790.

861 ——. *Versuch über die Vereinigung der musikalischen und oratorischen Declamation*. Berlin: Im Verlage der Musikhandlung und Musikdruckeren des Verfassers, [1786] (esp. recitative).

862 Remsen, Lester Ernest. "A Study of the Natural Trumpet and its Modern Counterpart," unpublished Ph.D. diss., University of Southern California, 1960 (natural vs. D valve trumpet).

862.01 Restout, Denise (ed.). *Landowska on Music*. New York: Stein and Day, 1964 (17–19th century keyboard; incl. bibliography).

862.02 Revitt, Paul J. "Domenico Corri's 'New System for Reading Thorough Bass,'" JAMS XXI (1968) 93–98 (realizations at the end of the 18th century).

863 Rey, Jean Baptiste. *Exposition Élémentaire de l'Harmonie. . . .* Paris: l'Auteur, [1807] (*b. c.*).

864 Richner, Thomas. *Orientation for Interpreting Mozart's Piano Sonatas*. New York: Bureau of Publications, Teachers College, Columbia University, 1953.

864.01 Riedel, Friedrich Wilhelm (ed.). Preface to Johann Joseph Fux's

Werke für Tasteninstrumente. Kassel: Bärenreiter, 1964 (fac. o. ornamentation tables by Gottlieb Muffat and P. P. Roskovsky).

864.02 Riemann, Hugo. "Beethoven als Clavierpädagog," MWb XXIV (1893) 541–42, 553–54, 569–70, 581–82 (incl. rhythm, accentuation, phrasing, technique, articulation).

865 ——. "Die Phrasierung im Lichte einer Lehre von den Tonvorstellungen," ZfMw I (1918–19) 26–39.

866 —— (ed.). Preface to *Mannheimer Kammermusik des 18. Jahrhunderts, I. Teil,* DTB XV (scordatura in Stamitz).

867 —— (ed.). Preface to *Sinfonien der Pfalzbayerischen Schule,* DTB III/1 (dynamics).

868 ——. "Tänze des 16. Jahrhunderts à double emploi," Mk VI/1 (1906–1907) 140–45.

868.01 Riemann, Margarete. "Die Überlieferung von Antonio de Cabezóns Klavierwerken und ihre Spiegelung in seinen Diferencias," AnM XXI (1966) 27–38 (repeats).

869 ——. "Zur Spielpraxis der Klaviervariation des 16. bis 18. Jahrhunderts," Mf VII (1954) 457–59.

870 Rigler, Franz Paul. *Anleitung zum Gesänge, und dem Klaviere, oder die Orgel zu spielen.* . . . Ofen: im Verlage der königl. hungar. Universitätsbuchdruckerey, 1798 (incl. ornamentation, *b. c.*).

871 Riley, Maurice Winton. "The Teaching of Bowed Instruments from 1511 to 1756," unpublished Ph.D. diss., University of Michigan, 1954 (incl. ornaments, bowing, fingerings, rhythms, pizzicato, mutes, double-stops, accompaniment).

872 Rinaldi, Mario. *Il Problema degli abbellimenti nell' op. V di Corelli.* Siena: Ticci, 1947.

873 Ritter, August Gottfried. *Zur Geschichte des Orgelspiels.* . . . Leipzig: M. Hesse, 1884.

873.01 Rochlitz, Friedrich. "Beiträge zur Lehre von den Verzierungen," AmZ XVI (1814) col. 125.

874 Rodolphe, Jean Joseph. *Théorie d'accompagnement et de composition.* . . . Paris: Chez le même, [1785] (*b. c.*).

875 Roeseler, Albrecht. *Studien zum Instrumentarium in den Vokalwerken von Heinrich Schütz: die obligaten Instrumente in den Psalmen Davids und in den Symphoniae sacrae I.* Berlin: Freie Universität, 1958.

876 Rognoni, Riccardo. *Passaggi per potersi essercitare nel diminuire terminatamente con ogni sorte d'Instrumenti, et anco diversi Passaggi per la semplice voce humana.* Venice: 1592.

877 Rokseth, Yvonne. "Instruments à l'Église au XVᵉ siècle," RM1 XIV (1933) 206–08.

877.001 Rose, Bernard. "Some Further Observations on the Performance of Purcell's Music," MT C (1959) 385–86 (incl. tempo, rhythm, ornamentation, *b. c.*).

877.01 Rose, Gloria. "Agazzari and the Improvising Orchestra," JAMS XVIII (1965) 382–93.

877.02 ——. "The Cantatas of Carissimi," unpublished Ph.D. diss., Yale University, 1960 (incl. ornamentation).

878 ——. "A Fresh Clue from Gasparini on Embellished Figured Bass Accompaniment," MT CVII (1966) 28–29 (Gasparini's *Cantata da camera a voce sola* [1695], incl. arias with realized accompaniments).

879 ——. "Polyphonic Italian Madrigals of the Seventeenth Century," ML XLVII (1966) 153–59 (incl. accompaniment).

880 Rosenkaimer, Eugen. "Das Saxophon in seinen Frühzeiten und im Urteil berühmter Musiker," Mk XX (1928) 896–900.

881 Rosenthal, Felix. "Probleme der musikalischen Metrik," ZfMw VIII (1925–26) 262–88 (esp. 19th century).

882 Rothschild, Fritz. *A Handbook to the Performance of the 48 Preludes and Fugues of J. S. Bach According to the Rules of the Old Tradition.* London: A. and C. Black, 1955 (rhythm, touch).

883 ——. *The Lost Tradition in Music: Rhythm and Tempo in J. S. Bach's Time.* London: A. and C. Black, 1953.

884 ——. "Mozart's Pianoforte Music—Some Aspects of Its Interpretation," *The Score* IX (1954) 3–11 (quotes Quantz, Czerny, and Marpurg; rhythm, tempo, articulation).

885 ——. *Musical Performance in the Times of Mozart and Beethoven: The Lost Tradition in Music Part II.* London: A. and C. Black, 1961 (incl. phrasing, dynamics, rhythm).

886 ——. "Rhythm and Tempo in Bach's Time," BAMS XI–XIII (1948) 27–28.

886.01 Rousseau, Eugene E. "Clarinet Instructional Materials from 1732 to *ca.* 1825," unpublished Ph.D. diss., State University of Iowa, 1962 (incl. fingerings, ornamentation, etc.).

887 Rousseau, Jean. *Méthode claire, certaine et facile, pour apprendre à chanter la musique,* 4th ed. Amsterdam: Estienne Roger, [n. d.] (incl. ornamentation, improvisation and articulation).

888 ——. *Traité de la viole.* Paris: Christophe Ballard, 1687 (incl. ornamentation, fingering, bowing, articulation).

889 Roussier, Pierre-Joseph. *L'Harmonie pratique.* . . . Paris: l'éditeur, [1775] (*b. c.*).

890 Rubsamen, Walter. "The Justiniane or Viniziane of the 15th Century," AMl XXIX (1957) 172–84 (improvisation).

891 Rücker, Ingeborg. *Die deutsche Orgel am Oberrhein um 1500.* Freiburg: Albert, 1940 (incl. texture and voicing).

892 Rückert, Heinz. "Zur Frage der Interpretation der Händel-Oper," Händel-Festspiele (1954) 27–30.

893 Rühlmann, Franz. "Zur Wiederbelebung Glucks," Festschrift STEIN 161–82 (opera).

894 Ruetz, Manfred. "Die Blockflöte in der Kirchenmusik Johann Sebastian Bachs," MuK VII (1935) 112–20, 170–86.

895 Ruhnke, Martin. *Joachim Burmeister: Ein Beitrag zur Musiklehre um 1600.* Kassel: Bärenreiter, 1955 (incl. conducting).

896 *Rules; or a Short and Compleat Method for Attaining to Play a Thorough Bass. . . .* London: Printed for and sold by I. Walsh, [17—] (incl. lexicon).

897 Rulhière, Claude Carloman de. *Jugement de l'orchestre de l'opéra.* [Paris?: n. p., 175–] (French vs. Italian styles).

897.01 Russell, John F. "Mozart and the Pianoforte," MR I (1940) 226–244 (esp. concertos).

897.02 Russell, Louis Arthur. *The Embellishments of Music.* Philadelphia: Theodore Presser, [1894] (chiefly late 18th and 19th centuries).

898 Russell, Raymond. *The Harpsichord and Clavichord: An Introductory Study.* London: Faber and Faber, 1959.

898.01 Russell, Theodore. "The Violin 'Scordatura,'" MQ XIV (1938) 84–96 (17th–19th centuries, when used).

S

899 Sabbatini, Galeazzo. *Regola facile, e breve per sonare sopra il Basso continuo. . . .* Venice: Salvatori, 1628.

900 Sachs, Curt. *Rhythm and Tempo. . . .* New York: W. W. Norton, 1953.

900.01 ——. "Chromatic Trumpets in the Renaissance," MQ XXXVI (1950) 62–66.

901 Saint-Foix, Georges de. "Considérations nouvelles sur quelques caractères ou éléments de l'Art Italien," RMl XXXVI (1954) 99–115 (incl. ornamentation).

902 Saint-Lambert, Michel de. *Nouveau traité de l'accompagnement. . . .* Paris: C. Ballard, 1707 (*b. c.*).

903 ——. *Les principes du clavecin. . . .* Paris: C. Ballard, 1702.

904 Saint-Sévin, Joseph Barnabé. *Principes du violon pour apprendre le doigté . . . et les différends agréments. . . .* Paris: Des Lauriers, [1761?] (incl. ornaments, fingering).

904.01 Sakka, Keisei. "Beethovens Klaviere," Festschrift SCHMIDT-GÖRG (70) 327–37.

905 Salmen, Walter. "Bemerkungen zum mehrstimmigen Musizieren der Spielleute im Mittelalter," RB XI (1957) 17–26 (instrumentation).

905.01 Salter, Humphry. *The Genteel Companion; Being exact Directions for the Recorder: . . .* London: printed for Richard Hunt & Humphry Salter, at the Lute in St. Paul's Church-Yard, 1683 (graces).

906 Salter, Sumner. "The Ornaments in Bach's Organ Works," MQ VI (1920) 392–402.

907 Salzer, Felix. "Über die Bedeutung der Ornamente in Philipp Emanuel Bachs Klavierwerken," ZfMw (1929–30) 398–418.

908 Samarelli, Francesco. "Josquino Salèpico vel Salèm da Molfetta, liutista e musicista del secolo XVI," *Note d'Archivio* IX (1932) 130–40.

908.01 Samber, Johann Baptist. *Continuatio ad Manuductionem Organicam.* . . . Salzburg: Johann Baptist Manes, 1702 (incl. registration, diminution) (cf. **908.02** and **908.03**).

908.02 ——. *Elucidatio musicae choralis.* . . . Salzburg: Johann Joseph Mayr, 171[0?] (cf. **908.01** and **911.01**).

908.03 ——. *Manuductio ad Organum.* . . . Salzburg: Johann Baptist Manes, 1704 (incl. *b. c.*, ornaments) (cf. **908.01** and **908.02**).

909 Sandberger, Adolf. "Notenbild und Werktreue," Festschrift STEIN 183–87.

910 Sander, Hans-Adolf. "Ein Orgelbuch der breslauer Magdalenenkirche aus dem 17. Jahrhundert; ein Beitrag zum Aufführungsbrauch des späten 16. und 17. Jahrhunderts," *Festschrift Max Schneider zum 60. Geburtstag überreicht von Kollegen, Freunden und Schülern,* ed. H. J. Zingel. Halle, Eisleben-Lutherstadt: E. Schneider, 1935 74–83.

910.01 Sands, Mollie. "The Decline and Revival of the Counter-tenor," MMR LXXXII (1952) 115–20.

911 Santa María, Fray Tomás de. *Libro llamado Arte de tañer Fantasia, assi para tecla como para Vihuela.* . . . Valladolid: Impresso por F. Fernandez de Cordoua, 1565 (improvisation).

911.01 Sargent, George. "Eighteenth Century Tuning Directions: Precise Intervallic Determination," MR XXX (1969) 27–34 (cf. **908.02**).

912 Sasse, Konrad. "Bemerkungen zur musikalischen Bearbeitungs- und Aufführungspraxis für Händels Opernwerke unter Berücksichtigung der Informationstheorie," Händel Jb (1963) 85–92.

913 Scarlatti, Alessandro. "Regole per cembalo," Brit. Mus. Add. MS. 14244, foll. 13, 38r–43v, and Add. MS. 31517, fol. 35, [ca. 1715].

914 Schacht, Matthias Henriksen. *Musicus Danicus eller Danske Sangmester,* Copenhagen Royal Library MS. Ny kgl. Saml. 109k, Fol. [Preface dated 1687]. Fac. Copenhagen: H. Hagerup, 1928 (incl. *b. c.*).

914.01 Schäffer, Julius. "Entgegnung auf Ph. Spitta's Artikel: 'Ueber das Accompagnement in den Compositionen Seb. Bach's,'" MWb VI (1875) 521–22, 533–36 (cf. **983.01** and **984.01**).

914.02 Scheibe, Johann Adolph. *Der critische Musicus.* Hamburg: issued irregularly, 1737–40 (general).

915 Scheidt, Samuel. Prefaces to *Tabulatura Nova für Orgel und Clavier,* DDT I (incl. registration, cantus firmus in pedal).

916 Schenk, Erich (ed.). Preface to Johann Joseph Fux's *Werke für Tasteninstrumente,* DTÖ LXXXV (ornamentation).

917 ——. "Zur Aufführungspraxis des Tremolo bei Gluck," *Anthony van*

Hoboken Festschrift zum 75. Geburtstag, ed. by J. Schmidt-Görg. Mainz: B. Schott's Söhne, (1962) 137–45.

918 Schenker, Heinrich. *Ein Beitrag zur Ornamentik als Einführung zu Ph. Em. Bachs Klavierwerken.* Vienna: Universal, 1908.

919 Schering, Arnold. *Aufführungspraxis alter Musik.* Leipzig: Quelle and Meyer, 1931.

920 ——. "Das kolorierte Orgelmadrigal des Trecento," SIMG XIII (1911–12) 172–204 (incl. scoring).

921 ——. "Die freie Kadenz im Instrumentalkonzert des 18. Jahrhunderts," *Bericht über den zweiten Kongress der Internationalen Musikgesellschaft zu Basel vom 25.–27. September, 1906.* Leipzig: Breitkopf & Härtel, 1907 204–11 (incl. ornamentation).

922 ——. "Musikalischer Organismus oder Deklamationsrhythmik?" ZfMw XI (1928–29) 212–21.

922.01 ——. *Die niederländische Orgelmesse im Zeitalter Josquins.* Leipzig: Breitkopf & Härtel, 1912 (incl. settings, ornamentation).

923 —— (ed.). Preface to *Instrumentalkonzerte deutscher Meister . . .*, DDT XXIX–XXX (improvisation of cadenzas, ornaments).

924 ——. "'Vorhalte' und 'Vorschläge' in Bachs Passionen und im Weinachtsoratorium," BJ XX (1923) 12–30.

925 ——. "Zur Choralrhythmik," KONGRESS 1925 (Leipzig) 365–67.

925.01 ——. "Zur Frage der Orgelmitwirkung in der Kirchenmusik des 15. Jahrhunderts," *Bericht über die Freiburger Tagung für deutsche Orgelkunst vom 27. bis 30. Juli 1926,* ed. by W. Gurlitt. Augsburg: Bärenreiter, 1926 87–91 (role of the organ).

926 ——. "Zur instrumentalen Verzierungskunst im 18. Jahrhundert," SIMG VII (1905–06) 365–85.

927 ——. "Zur Orgelmesse," ZIMG XV (1913–14) 11–16 (cf. Leichtentritt, "Einige Bermerkungen . . ." and "Zur 'Orgelmesse' . . .").

928 Scherlich, Norbert. "Zur Frage der Gesangsappoggiatur," Österr MZ XVIII (1963) 283–91.

929 Schierning, Lydia. *Die Überlieferung der deutschen Orgel- und Klaviermusik aus der 1. Hälfte des 17. Jahrhunderts.* Kassel: Bärenreiter-Verlag, 1961.

930 Schilling, Hans Ludwig. "Zur Instrumentenwahl in der Continuopraxis," SMZ XCVIII (1958) 6–9.

931 Schlecht, Raymond. "Ein Beitrag zur Musikgeschichte aus dem Anfange des 16. Jahrhunderts, nach dem 'Spiegel der Orgelmacher und Organisten von Arnold Schlick,' 1511," MfM II (1870) 165–76, 181–88, 197–207 (tuning, registration, accompaniment).

932 ——. "Über die Tonhöhe u. Schreibweise der Kompositionen aus dem 15. und 16. Jahrhunderte," MfM III (1871) 117–26 (vocal music).

933 Schlenger, Kurt. "Über Verwendung und Notation der Holzblasinstrumente in den frühen Kantaten Joh. Seb. Bachs," BJ XXVIII (1931) 88–106.

934 Schlick, Arnolt. "Spiegel der Orgelmacher und Organisten," reprint in Mf M I (1869) 77–114.

935 Schmid, Ernst Fritz. "Joseph Haydn und die vokale Zierpraxis seiner Zeit, dargestellt an einer Arie seines Tobias-Oratoriums," *Bericht über die Internationale Konferenz zum Andenken Joseph Haydns*, ed. B. Szabolcsi and D. Bartha. Budapest: Akadémiai Kiadó, 1961 117–29.

936 Schmidt, Christopher. "Philipp Emanuel Bach und das Clavichord," SMZ XCII (1952) 441–46.

937 Schmidt, Ferdinand. "Wechselgesang—Seine Anwendung und Ausführung im Evangelischen Gottesdienst," MuK VII (1935) 36–41, 54–58.

938 Schmitz, Arnold. "Die Kadenz als Ornamentum musicae," KONGRESS 1953 (Bamberg) 114–20.

939 Schmitz, Hans-Peter. *Die Kunst der Verzierung im 18. Jahrhundert*. Kassel: Bärenreiter-Verlag, 1955.

940 ——. *Prinzipien der Aufführungspraxis alter Musik*. Berlin: Knauer-Verlag, [1950] (esp. keyboard).

941 ——. *Querflöte und Querflötenspiel in Deutschland während des Barockzeitalters*. Kassel: Bärenreiter-Verlag, 1952.

942 ——. "Über die Verwendung von Querflöten des 18. Jahrhunderts in unserer Zeit," Festschrift SCHNEIDER (80) 277–84.

942.01 Schneider, Friedrich. *Handbuch des Organisten*, 3 vols. Halberstadt: bei Carl Brüggemann, 1829–30 (incl. fingering, ornamentation, expression, *b. c.*).

943 Schneider, Max. *Die Anfänge des Basso continuo und seiner Bezifferung*. Leipzig: Breitkopf & Härtel, 1918.

944 ——. "Die Begleitung des Secco-Rezitativs um 1750," Gluck Jb (1917) 88–107.

944.01 ——. *Beiträge zu einer Anleitung Clavichord und Cembalo zu spielen*. Strassburg: Heitz & Co., 1934 (general—based on historical information).

945 ——. "Die Besetzung der vielstimmigen Musik des 17. und 16. Jahrhunderts," AfMw I (1919) 205–34.

946 ——. "Der Generalbass Johann Sebastian Bachs," JbP XXI–XXII (1914–15) 27–42.

947 Schneider, Michael. *Die Orgelspieltechnik des frühen 19. Jahrhunderts in Deutschland, dargestellt an den Orgelschulen der Zeit. . . .* Regensburg: Bosse, 1941.

947.001 Schoenleben, Anne. "Performance Practices at San Petronio in the Baroque," AMl XLI (1969) 37–55.

947.01 Scholl, Evelyn H. "New Light on 17th-Century Pronunciation of the English School of Lutenist Song Writers," *Modern Language Association Publications* LIX (1944) 398–445.

948 Schrade, Leo (ed.). Preface to *La Représentation D'Edipo Tiranno Au Teatro Olimpico* (*Vicence, 1585*). Paris: Éditions du Centre National de la Recherche Scientifique, 1960 (incl. singing style).

949 ——. "Sulla natura del ritmo barocco," RMI LVI (1954) 3–27.

950 Schreiber, Ottmar. *Orchester und Orchesterpraxis in Deutschland zwischen 1780 und 1850.* Berlin: Triltsch und Luther, 1938.

951 Schroeder, Rolph. "Über das Problem des mehrstimmigen Spiels in J.S. Bachs Violinsolosonaten," Festschrift BACH-PROBLEME 74–80.

952 Schröter, Christoph Gottlieb. *Deutliche Anweisung zum General-Bass . . . .* Halberstadt: J. H. Gross, 1772.

952.01 Schubert, Johann Friedrich. *Neue Singe-Schule. . . .* Leipzig: Breit-kopf & Härtel, [1804] (esp. ornamentation, cadenzas, impro-visation, dynamics).

953 Schünemann, Georg. *Geschichte des Dirigierens.* Leipzig: Breitkopf & Härtel, 1913.

954 —— (ed.). Die Quellen in *Trompeterfanfaren Sonaten und Feldstücke,* EdM VII (incl. articulation, range).

955 ——. "Zur Frage des Taktschlagens und der Textbehandlung in der Mensuralmusik," SIMG X (1908–09) 73–114.

955.01 Schütze, Friedrich Wilhelm. *Handbuch zu der praktischen Orgelschule.* Leipzig: Arnoldische Buchhandlung, 1868 (general).

955.02 Schwandt, Erich P. "The Ornamented Clausula Diminuta in the Fitzwilliam Virginal Book," unpublished Ph.D. diss., Stanford University, 1967.

956 Schwartz, Rudolf. "Zur Geschichte des Taktschlagens," JbP XIV (1907) 59–70 (17th–18th centuries).

957 Schwarz, Gerhard. "Die Improvisation als handwerkliche Kunst und Aufgabe für den Kirchenmusiker," MuK VI (1934) 32–41 (esp. chorale preludes).

958 Schweiger, Hertha. "Abbé G. J. Voglers Orgellehre. Ein Beitrag zur Klanggeschichte der frühromantischen Orgel," unpublished Ph.D. diss., Freiburg, 1938 (texture and voicing).

959 Schweitzer, Albert. "Der für Bachs Werke für Violine solo erforder-liche Geigenbogen," Bachgedenkschrift 75–83 (bowing).

959.01 Scott, Marion M. "Solo Violin Sonatas," ML X (1929) 46–57 (incl. scordatura, bowing, ornamentation through 18th century).

960 Seagrave, Barbara Anne Garvey. "The French Style of Violin Bowing and Phrasing from Lully to Jacques Aubert (1650–1730)," unpublished Ph.D. diss., Stanford University, 1958.

960.01 Seidl, Arthur. "Der Mordent im 'Rienzi,'" MWb XXV (1894) 481–82, 493–94.

961 Seiffert, Max. "Bildzeugnisse des 16. Jahrhunderts für die instrumentale Begleitung des Gesanges und den Ursprung des Musikkupferstiches," AfMw I (1918–19) 49–67 (iconography).

961.01 ——. *Geschichte der Klaviermusik.* Leipzig: Breitkopf & Härtel, 1899 (comprehensive, to 1750).

962 —— (ed.). Preface to Johann Gottfried Walther's *Gesammelte Werke für Orgel,* DDT XXVI–XXVII (incl. registration).

963 ——. "Die Verzierung der Sologesänge in Händels *Messias,*" SIMG VIII (1906–07) 581–615.

964 Selbiger, Liselotte. "Bach on the Piano," MR XI (1950) 98–108 (incl. dynamics, articulation, phrasing, fingering).

964.01 Severi, Francesco. *Arie da cantarsi nel Chitarrone.* . . . Rome: Paolo Masotti, 1626 (vocal embellishment).

965 ——. *Salmi passaggiati per tutte le voci* . . . , Libro I. Rome: Nicolò Borboni, 1615 (embellishment).

965.01 Shaw, Watkins. "Covent Garden Performances of *Messiah* in 1749, 1752 and 1753," MR XIX (1958) 85–93 (aria settings).

965.02 ——. "Handel's *Messiah*: A Study of Selected Contemporary Word-Books," MQ XLV (1959) 208–22 (on Handel's own performances).

965.03 ——. "Purcell's 'Bell' Anthem and its Performance," MT C (1959) 285—86 (tempo, rhythm, ornamentation).

965.04 Sherlock, William. *A Sermon Preach'd at St. Paul's Cathedral, Nov. 22, 1699.* London: W. Rogers, 1699 (use of instruments in church).

965.05 Silva, Paulo do Couto e. *Da Interpretação Musical.* Rio de Janeiro: Editôra Globo, 1960 (general).

966 Simon, James. "Die Orchesterbehandlung in Mozarts Opern von Idomeneo bis zur Zauberflöte," Mk XIV (1914–15) 3–26, 61–79.

966.01 Simonds, Bruce. "Chopin's Use of the Term 'Con Anima.'" MTNA Proceedings XLII (1948) 515–57.

967 Simpson, Christopher. *The Division-Violist: or, an Introduction to the Playing upon a Ground.* London: 1659. 2nd ed. as *Chelys, minuritionum artificio exornata* . . . *The Division-Viol.* London: W. Godbid, 1667. Fac. of 2nd ed. by N. Dolmetsch. London: J. Curwen, 1955 (incl. *b. c.,* diminution).

968 ——. *The Principles of Practical Musick.* London: Printed by W. Godbid for H. Brome, 1665. [Later eds. under titles *A Compendium of Practical Musick* and *A Compendium: or, Introduction to Practical Musick*] (singing, instruments, figurate descant).

969 [Simpson, John (printer)]. *The Compleat Tutor for the Flute.* . . . London: John Simpson, [17—] (recorder).

969.01 "Sing-Schule," MS L. C. MT 840.S4 [n. d.] (esp. realized ornaments, articulation, phrasing, dynamics, etc.).

89

970 Skapski, George Joseph. "'Recitar Suonando?'" *Paul A. Pisk: Essays in His Honor*, ed. J. Glowacki. Austin: College of Fine Arts, University of Texas, 1966 82–95 (vocal and instrumental).

971 Śliwiński, Zbigniew. "Ein Beitrag zum Thema: Ausführung der Vorschläge in W. A. Mozarts Klavierwerken," Mozart Jb (1965–1966) 179–94.

972 Smethergell, William. *Rules for Thorough Bass, To which are annex'd, Three Sonatas*. . . . London: F. Linley, [179–] (incl. realizations).

972.01 Smiles, Joan Ellen. "Improvised Ornamentation in Late Eighteenth-Century Music," unpublished Ph.D. diss., Stanford University, [1969].

973 Smithers, Don. "Seventeenth-Century English Trumpet Music," ML XLVIII (1967) 358–65 (incl. instrumentation).

973.01 Smoldon, W. L. "The Music of the Medieval Church Drama," MQ XLVIII (1962) 476–97 (last eight pages deal with instrumental accompaniment).

974 Sočnik, Hugo. "Die zeitgenössische Überlieferung der Beethoven-Interpretation," AfMw XI (1954) 60–64 (quotes Czerny, Moscheles, *et al.*).

975 Solano, Francisco Ignacio. *Novo Tratado de musica metrica, e rythmica*. . . . Lisbon: Na Regia officina typografica, 1779 (*b. c.*).

976 Solerti, Angelo (comp. and ed.). *Le Origini del melodramma: Testimonianze dei contemporanei*. Turin: Fratelli Bocca, 1903 (incl. dedications and prefaces to Italian Baroque vocal music).

977 Sondheimer, Robert. "Art und Aufführungsstil vorklassischer Sinfonien," Mk XXIII (1931) 344–50.

977.01 ——. "On Performing Beethoven's Third and Fifth Symphonies," MR II (1941) 36–62 (esp. tempo, rhythm).

977.02 Sorge, Georg Andreas. *Anleitung zur fantasie, oder zu der schönen Kunst das Clavier*. . . . Lobenstein: im Verlag des Verfassers, [1767].

978 ——. *Compendium harmonicum*. . . . Lobenstein: Im Verlag des Verfassers, und in Commission in Hof bey Ludwig, [1760] (*b. c.*).

979 ——. *Vorgemach der musicalischen Composition*. . . . Lobenstein: Im Verlag des Autoris, [1745–47] (*b. c.*).

980 Spazier, Johann Gottlieb Karl (ed.). *Berlinische musikalische Zeitung*. Berlin: Im Verlage der neuen Musikhandlung, 1794 (periodical, general).

981 Speer, Daniel. *Grund-richtiger, Kurtz-, Leicht-, und nöthiger, jetzt Wolvermehrter Unterricht der Musicalischen Kunst*. . . . Ulm: in Verlag Georg Wilhelm Kühnen, 1697 (*b. c.*).

982 Speer, Klaus. "Die Artikulation in den Orgelwerken Joh. Seb. Bachs," BJ XLI (1954) 66–74.

982.01 Sperling, Johann Peter. *Principia Musicae*, . . . Budissin: Andreas Richtern, 1705 (voice).

90

982.02 Spink, Ian. "Playford's 'Directions for Singing After the Italian Manner,'" MMR LXXXIX (1959) 130–35.

983 Spitta, Friedrich. "Die Passionen von Schütz und ihre Wiederbelebung," JbP XIII (1906) 15–28.

983.01 Spitta, Phillipp. "Schlusswort über das Accompagnement und die Ansichten J. Schäffer's," MWb VI (1875) 549–51 (cf. **914.01** and **984.01**).

984 ——. "Über das Accompagnement in den Compositionen Sebastian Bachs," AmZ X (1875) 721–29, 740–45.

984.01 ——. "Über das Accompagnement in den Compositionen Seb. Bach's," MWb VI (1875) 489–93, 505–08 (*b. c.*) (cf. **914.01** and **983.01**).

985 Spohr, Louis. *Violinschule*. Vienna: T. Haslinger, [c. 1832]. Fac. F. Göthel. Kassel: 1960. Eng. trans. by C. Rudolphus as *Louis Spohr's Grand Violin School*. . . . London: Wessel & Co., [18—].

986 Springer, Hermann. "Der Anteil der Instrumentalmusik an der Literatur des 14.-16. Jahrhunderts," ZIMG XIII (1911–12) 265–69.

987 Squire, William Barclay. "Purcell as Theorist," SIMG VI (1904–05) 521–67 (incl. tempo, rhythm, *b. c.*, ornamentation).

988 Staden, Johann. "Kurzer und einfältiger Bericht für diejenigen, so im Basso ad Organum unerfahren," *Kirchen-Music, Ander Theil*. Nuremberg: 1626. Reprinted in AmZ XII (1877) 99 f. (*b. c.*).

989 Stadlen, Peter. "Beethoven and the Metronome," ML XLVIII (1967) 330–49.

990 Stainer, John and Cecie Stainer (ed.). Preface to *Dufay and His Contemporaries*. . . . London: Novello, 1898 (incl. instrumental accompaniment).

991 Starkey, Willard A. "The History and Practice of Ensemble Music for Lip-Reed Instruments," unpublished Ph.D. diss., State University of Iowa, 1954.

992 Steglich, Rudolf. "Das Ausziehrungswesen in der Musik W. A. Mozarts," Mozart Jb (1955) 181–237.

993 ——. "Interpretationsprobleme der Jupitersinfonie," Mozart Jb (1954) 102–12 (tempo, articulation, dynamics).

994 ——. "Nochmals: Über die Generalbassbegleitung zu Kammermusikwerken Bachs," Mf X (1957) 422–23 (cf. Oberdörffer, "Über . . . Spätbarock," and, "Über . . . Schlusswort . . . .").

994.01 ——. "Nochmals Verzierungskunst und Kontratanz," *Hausmusik* XV (1951) 84–86.

995 —— (ed.). Preface to C. P. E. Bach's *Preussischen Sonaten für Klavier*, *Nr. 1–3*, Nagel IV (ornamentation).

996 —— (ed.). Preface to C. P. E. Bach's *Würtemburgischen Sonaten, Nr. 1–3 und 4–6*, Nagel XXI–XXII (ornamentation).

997 ——. "Studien an Mozarts Hammerflügel," Neues Mozart Jb (1941) 181–210.

998 ——. "Das Tempo als Problem der Mozartinterpretation," *Bericht über die musikwissenschaftliche Tagung der Internationalen Stiftung Mozarteum in Salzburg*, ed. E. Schenk. Leipzig: Breitkopf & Härtel, 1932 172–79.

999 ——. "Über Mozarts Adagio-Takt," Mozart Jb (1951) 90–111.

1000 ——. "Zur Aufführung der Johannespassion J. S. Bachs," MuK XXVII (1957) 94–102 (incl. tempo, dynamics).

1001 ——. "Zwei Titelzeichnungen zu Robert Schumanns Jugendalbum als Interpretationsdokumente," *Deutsches Jahrbuch der Musikwissenschaft* (1959) 38–47 (incl. tempo).

1002 Stendhal [Beyle, Henri]. "L'opéra italien en 1826," RM (Aug., 1921) 113–31 (20 critiques from "Journal de Paris").

1003 Stephan, Rudolf. "Über das Ende der Generalbasspraxis," BJ XLI (1954) 80–88.

1004 ——. "Die vox alta bei Bach," MuK XXIII (1953) 58–65.

1005 Stevens, Denis. "Another View of the Bach Bow," MT XCVI (1955) 98 (cf. **58**, **1029**, **1030**, **1031**).

1006 —— (ed.). *The Art of Ornamentation and Embellishment in the Renaissance and Baroque*. New York: Vanguard Records BGS 70697/8 (Stereo), 1967.

1007 ——. "Ornamentation in Monteverdi's Shorter Dramatic Works," KONGRESS 1958 (Cologne) 284–87.

1008 ——. "Problems of Editing and Publishing Old Music," KONGRESS 1961 (New York) 150–58.

1008.01 ——. "The Role Played by Instruments," *Tudor Church Music*, rev. ed. New York: W. W. Norton, 1966 64–75 (esp. use of organ).

1009 Stevenson, Robert. *Juan Bermudo*. The Hague: M. Nijhoff, 1960 (incl. bibliography, ornamentation, tempo).

1010 Stilz, Ernst. "Über harmonische Ausfüllung in der Klaviermusik des Rokoko," ZfMw XIII (1930–31) 11–20 (texture).

1011 Stockhammer, Robert. "Die Kadenzen zu den Klavierkonzerten der Wiener Klassiker," unpublished Ph.D. diss., Vienna, 1936.

1011.01 Stockhausen, J. "Die Vorschläge im Dienst der Rhythmus," AMz XVI (1900) 667, 685, 701.

1012 Strub, Max. "Künstlerische Probleme im Alltag des Geigers," Festschrift RAABE 229–34 (incl. bowing, ornaments).

1013 Strunk, Oliver. *Source Readings in Music History*. New York: W. W. Norton, 1950.

1014 Stute, Heinrich. "Studien über den Gebrauch der Instrumente in dem italienischen Kirchenorchester des 18. Jahrhunderts. Ein Beitrag zur Geschichte der instrumental begleiteten Messe in Italien

...," unpublished Ph.D. diss., Münster, 1930 (incl. technique, ensemble, dynamics, phrasing).

1015 Sumner, William L. "The Baroque Organ," PRMA LXXXI (1954–1955) 1–12.

1016 ———. *The Organ: Its Evolution, Principles of Construction, and Use*. New York: Philosophical Library, 1952 (incl. articulation, pedaling, registration).

1016.01 Sutton, Julia. "The Lute Instructions of Jean-Baptiste Besard," MQ LI (1965) 345–62.

1016.02 Swainson, Dorothy. "'Silences d'articulation,'" *The Consort* No. 5 (1948) 13–16.

1016.03 ———. "The Turn," *The Consort* No. 11 (1954) 38–40 (quotes Mozart).

1016.04 ———. "The 'Upper Mordent,'" *The Consort* No. 8 (1951) 16–18 (18th century).

1017 Swaryczewska, Katarzyna. "The Performing Practice in Poland up to the XVIII Century," *Polish Music*, ed. by S. Jarociński. Warsaw: Polish Scientific Publishers, 1965 65–79 (instrumental and choral dispositions by eras and performing groups).

1018 [Symposium]. "Dynamik und Agogik in der Musik des Barock," KONGRESS 1958 (Cologne) 343–49.

1019 [———]. "Performance Practice in the 17th and 18th Centuries," KONGRESS 1961 (New York) 220–35 (incl. *notes inégales*, dotted rhythm, dynamics, instrumentation).

1019.01 [———]. "Schubert as Written and As Performed: A Symposium," MT CIV (1963) 626–28 (*Die Winterreise*; rhythm, tempo).

1020 Szabolcsi, Benedikt. "Über Kulturkreise der musikalischen Ornamentik in Europa," ZfMw XVII (1935) 65–82.

T

1020.01 Tacchinardi, Guido. *Studio sulla Interpretazione della Musica*. Florence: Tipografia Galletti & Cecci, 1902 (after 1750).

1020.02 Taggart, James Leland. "Franz Schubert's Piano Sonatas: A Study of Performance Problems," unpublished Ph.D. diss., State University of Iowa, 1963 (order of movements, phrasing, articulation, dynamics, accentuation, ornaments, tempo).

1021 Tagliavini, Luigi Ferdinando (ed.). Preface to *Sonate d'Intavolatura per Organo e Cimbalo*. Heidelberg: Willy Müller, 1959 (registration, ornamentation).

1022 Tans'ur, William. *A New Musical Grammar*. . . . London: J. Robinson, 1746 (vocal, instrumental).

1023 Tartini, Giuseppe. *L'Arte dell' arco o siano cinquanta variazioni*. Naples: Marescalchi, [?1750]. Incl. in J.-B. Cartier's *L'art du violon*. 2nd ed., Paris: Decombe, 1798 (free ornamentation of Corelli gavotte).

1024 ——. *A Letter from the Late Signor Tartini to Signora Maddalena Lombardini, (Now Signora Sirmen)*, trans. by Dr. Burney. London: Printed for R. Bremner by G. Bigg, 1779. Fac. New York: Johnson Reprint Corp., 1967 (violin).

1025 ——. *Traité des agréments de la musique* . . ., trans. by P. Denis. Paris: l'auteur, [1782]. Ed. by E. R. Jacobi, with Eng. trans. by C. Girdlestone and fac. of original It. text. Celle: H. Moeck, [1961]. Eng. trans. by S. Babitz as "Treatise on the Ornamentation," JRME IV (1956) 75–102. Reprinted by Carl Fischer [1957?].

1025.01 Tatnell, Roland Stuart. "Falsetto Practice: A Brief Survey," *The Consort* No. 22 (1965) 31–35.

1026 Telemann, Georg Michael. *Unterricht im Generalbass-Spielen.* . . . Hamburg: Michael Christian Bock, 1773.

1027 Telemann, Georg Philipp. Preface to *Harmonischer Gottes-Dienst, oder geistliche Cantaten.* [Hamburg: In Verlegung des Autoris, und bey demselben, auch in den Leipziger-Messen im kissnerischen Buch-Laden zu finden, 1725–26]. Ed. by G. Fock in *Georg Philipp Telemann: Musikalische Werke*, Vol. II Kassel: Bärenreiter-Verlag, 1953 (incl. instrumentation, tempo, recitatives).

1028 ——. *Singe-, Spiel- und Generalbass-Übungen.* [Hamburg: issued in installments, from Nov. 20, 1733, to Jan. 17, 1735]. Ed. M. Seiffert, 3rd ed. Berlin: Leo Liepmannssohn, 1927.

1029 Telmányi, Emil. "Lösung der Probleme der Solo-Violinwerke von Bach," SMZ XCV (1955) 430–34 (Vega bow).

1030 ——. "The Purpose of the 'Vega-Bach-Bow.' A reply to Mr. Denis Stevens and Mr. Sol Babitz," MT XCVI (1955) 371–72.

1031 ——. "Some Problems in Bach's Unaccompanied Violin Music," MT XCVI (1955) 14–18 (bowing and fingering, Vega bow) (cf.: **58**, **1005**, **1029**, **1030**).

1031.01 Temperly, Nicholas. "Tempo and Repeats in the Early 19th Century," ML XLVII (1966) 323–36 (quotes Smart's performance timings).

1031.02 Tenducci, Giusto Ferdinando. *Instruction of Mr. Tenducci to his Scholars.* [London]: Longman & Broderip, [1785] (comprehensive; incl. written-out ornaments).

1031.03 [Terrasson, Antoine]. *Dissertation historique sur la vielle.* . . . Paris: chez J. B. Lamasle, 1741 (occasion for use, up to 1700).

1031.04 Terry, Charles Sanford. "Bach's Kettledrums," MT LXXII (1931) 119–21.

1032 ——. *Bach's Orchestra.* London: Oxford University Press, [1932].

1032.01 Testori, Carlo Giovanni. *La musica ragionata espressa famigliarmente in dodici passegiate a dialogo*; . . . Vercelli: G. Panialis, 1767 (cf. **1032.02**).

1032.02 ——. *Primi rudimenti della musica e supplemento alla Musica ragionata.*
. . . Vercelli: G. Panialis, 1771 (cf. **1032.01**).

1033 Thalheimer, Peter. "Der Flauto piccolo bei Johann Sebastian Bach,"
BJ LII (1966) 138–46.

1033.01 Thibault, Geneviève. "L'Ornamentation dans la musique profane
au Moyen-Age," KONGRESS 1961 (New York) 450–63
(through 16th century).

1034 Thoene, Walter. "Zur Frage der Artikulation im Cembalo- und
Clavichordspiel," Festschrift FELLERER 535–48.

1035 Thomas, Kurt. "Gedanken zur Aufführungspraxis der Chorwerke von
J. S. Bach," *Das Musikleben* III (1950) 33–37 (incl. instrumentation, chorales, fermatas, arias, recitatives).

1036 ——. "Zur Chorleiter- und Dirigentenerziehung," Festschrift STEIN
129–34.

1037 Thomson, Ulf. "Voraussetzungen und Artung der österreichischen
Generalbasslehre zwischen Albrechtsberger und Sechter," unpublished Ph.D. diss., Vienna, 1960.

1038 *Thorough Bass At One View With Directions for Accompaniment And Proper
Examples.* [London]: Printed at Thompson's Warehouse,
[17—] (incl. realizations).

1038.01 Thürmer, Helmut. "Zum Deklamationsproblem im deutschen
Sololied," Festschrift SCHMIDT-GÖRG (70) 386–93 (19th
century).

1039 Tinctoris, Johannes. *De inventione et usu musicae.* [Naples?: 1487?]. Reprint in K. Weinmann, *Johannes Tinctoris und sein unbekannter
Traktat "De inventione et usu musicae,"* 2nd ed. Tutzing: H.
Schneider, 1961. Partial Eng. trans. by A. Baines in GSJ III
(1950) 19–26.

1040 Titcomb, Caldwell. "Carrousel Music at the Court of Louis XIV,"
Festschrift DAVISON 205–13 (equestrian ballet).

1041 Tomeoni, Florido. *Théorie de la musique vocale.* Paris: Charles Pougens,
1799 (incl. ornamentation).

1041.01 Toni, Alceo. *Studi critici di interpretazione.* Milan: Bottega di Poesia,
1925 (general).

1042 ——. "Sul basso continuo e l'interpretazione della Musica antica,"
RMI XXVI (1919) 229–64.

1043 Torchi, Luigi. "L'accompagnamento degl' Istrumenti nei Melodrammi
italiani della prima metà del Seicento," RMI I (1894) 7–38.

1044 Torres y Martínez Bravo, José de. *Reglas generales de acompañar.* . . .
Madrid: En la Imprenta de mvsica, 1702 (*b. c.*).

1045 Tosi, Pier Francesco. *Opinioni de' cantori antichi, e moderni.* . . . [Bologna:
L. dalla Volpe, 1723]. Eng. trans. by J. E. Galliard as *Observa-
tions on the Florid Song* . . . , 2nd ed. London: J. Wilcox, 1743.
Fac. London: W. Reeves, 1926. Ger. trans. and annot. by
J. F. Agricola *Anleitung* as *zur Singkunst.* . . . Berlin: G. L. Winter,

95

1757. Fac. ed. by E. R. Jacobi. Celle: Hermann Moeck Verlag, 1966 (incl. ornamentation, improvisation).

1046 [Treiber, Johann Philipp]. *Der accurate Organist im General-Bass.* Jena: 1704.

1047 Tretick, Sidney James. "An Analysis of Performance Practices for the Johann Sebastian Bach Chaconne Based Upon the Anna Magdalena Manuscript," unpublished D.M.A. diss., University of Colorado, 1957.

1047.01 Tromlitz, Johann George. *Ausführlicher und grundlicher Unterricht die Flöte zu spielen.* Leipzig: Adam Friedrich Boehme, 1791 (comprehensive).

1048 Trydell, the Rev. John, *Two Essays on the Theory and Practice of Music.* . . . Dublin: Boulter Grierson, 1766 (incl. *b. c.*).

1049 Türk, Daniel Gottlob. *Klavierschule, oder Anweisung zum Klavierspielen für Lehrer und Lernende.* . . . Leipzig and Halle: Auf Kosten des Verfassers, in Kommission bey Schwickert in Leipzig, 1789. Fac. ed. by E. R. Jacobi. Kassel: Bärenreiter, 1962. Eng. trans. and abrid. by C. G. Naumburger as *Treatise on the Art of Teaching and Practicing the Pianoforte.* London: [1804] (incl. ornamentation, fingering, tempo, cadenzas).

1050 ——. *Kurze Anweisung zum Generalbass-Spielen.* . . . Halle and Leipzig: Auf Kosten des Verfassers, in Kommission bey Schwickert, 1791.

1051 ——. *Von den wichtigsten Pflichten eines Organisten.* Halle: Auf kosten des Verfassers, in Kommission bei Schwickert zu Leipzig, 1787.

1051.01 Tureck, Rosalyn. "Bach in the Twentieth Century," MT CIII (1962) 92–95 (keyboard instrumentation, tempo).

1052 ——. *An Introduction to the Performance of Bach,* 3 vols. London: Oxford University Press, 1960 (incl. ornamentation, phrasing, articulation).

1053 Tutenberg, Fritz. "Werktreue bei der Operninszenierung," Festschrift STEIN 188–95.

1053.01 Tyson, Alan. "The Textual Problems of Beethoven's Violin Concerto," MQ LIII (1967) 482–502.

U

1054 Ulrich, Ernst. *Studien zur deutschen Generalbass-Praxis in der ersten Hälfte des 18. Jahrhunderts.* Kassel: Bärenreiter-Verlag, 1932 (incl. bibliography).

1055 Unger, Robert. *Die mehrchörige Aufführungspraxis bei Michael Praetorius und die Feiergestaltung der Gegenwart.* Wolfenbüttel: Kallmeyer, 1941.

1056 Ursprung, Otto. "Die Chorordnung von 1616 am Dom zu Augsburg; Ein Beitrag zur Frage der Aufführungspraxis," Festschrift ADLER 137–42.

1057 Vaccaj, Nicola. *Metodo pratico per il canto italiano.* Milan: Ricordi, [n. d.]. Eng. trans. by J. C. D. Parker. Boston: G. D. Russell & Co., 1865.

1058 Van den Borren, Charles. "Orlande de Lassus et la Musique instrumentale," RM III, no. 7 (May, 1922) 111–26 (instrumentation).

1059 ——. "La pureté du style et l'interprétation de la musique du Moyen-Age," *La Revue Internationale de Musique* I (1938) 96–102, 273–79.

1060 —— and Safford Cape. "Autour du 'Tactus,'" RB VIII (1954) 41–45 (Dufay).

1061 Vander Linden, Albert. "A propos du 'Lauda Sion' de Mendelssohn," RB XVII (1963) 124–25 (tempo).

1062 Van der Straeten, Edmund Sebastian Joseph. "Some Remarks by Beethoven with Regard to the Performance of his Works," MMR XXVII (1897) 3–6, 79–80 (tempo).

1062.01 Vanderwerf, Hendrik. "Deklamatorischer Rhythmus in den Chansons der Trouvères," Mf XX (1967) 122–44.

1063 Van Ess, Donald Harrison. "The Stylistic Evolution of the English Brass Ensemble," unpublished Ph.D. diss., Boston University, 1963.

1064 Vaughan Williams, Ralph (ed.). Preface to Henry Purcell's *Complete Works*, Vol. XV. London: Novello, 1905 (ornaments).

1064.01 Vennum, Thomas, Jr. "The Registration of Frescobaldi's Organ Music," *Organ Institute Quarterly* XI/1 (1964) 14–19 and XI/2 (1964) 1–11 (incl. bibliography).

1065 Vente, Maarten Albert. "Mitteilungen über iberische Registrierkunst unter besonderer Berücksichtigung der Orgelkompositionen des Juan Cabanilles," AnM XVII (1962) 41–62.

1066 Venturini, Giorgio. "Del modo di rappresentare le opere del passato e dell' *Amfiparnaso* di Orazio Vecchi," KONGRESS 1938 (Florence) 108–13.

1067 *Vermehrter und nun zum zweytenmal in Druck beförderter.* . . . Augsburg: J. Koppmayer, 1693 (incl. *b. c.*, G. Carissimi).

1068 [Viadana, Lodovico (da)]. "Lodovico Viadana's *Vorrede* von 1620 mit 2 Tonsätzen," MfM VIII (1876) 105–10 (*b. c.*).

1069 ——. Preface to *Cento concerti ecclesiastici.* . . . Venice: Giacomo Vincenti, 1602. Mod. ed. Kassel: Bärenreiter, 1964 (incl. *b. c.*).

1069.01 Vierling, Johann Gottfried. *Versuch einer Anleitung zum Präludiren.* . . . new ed. Leipzig: Breitkopf & Härtel, [1794] (keyboard).

1069.02 Vogan, Charles Edward. "French Organ School of the 17th and 18th Centuries," unpublished Ph.D. diss., University of Michigan, 1949 (esp. Appendices B and C: registration and ornamentation).

1070 Vogel, Emil. "Zur Geschichte des Taktschlagens," JbP V (1898) 67–76.

1071 Vogel, Jaroslav. "On the Interpretation of Janáček's Works," *Leoš Janáček: His Life and Works*. London: Hamlyn, 1962 399–409 (incl. ensemble, dynamics).

1071.01 Vogler, Georg Joseph. *Stimmbildungskunst.* Mannheim: Hofbuchdruckerei, 1776 (incl. realized diminutions).

1072 Voigt, Wilhelm. "Erfahrungen und Ratschläge bezüglich der Aufführung Bachscher Kirchenkantaten," BJ III (1906) 1–42.

1073 Volbach, Fritz. "Die Grundzüge der Anwendung und Bedeutung der Koloratur bei Händel und Chrysanders Stellung zu derselben," AMz XXV (1898) 421–22, 437–40, 453–55, 469–70.

1074 ———. "Die Praxis der Händel-Aufführung," unpublished Ph.D. diss., Bonn, 1899 (instrumentation).

1074.01 Volek, Tomislav. "Die erste Aufführung der 'Zauberflöte' in tschechischer Sprache in Prag 1794," Mozart Jb (1967) 387–91.

1075 von Brescius, Hans. "Die Kapelle zur Zeit Reissigers und Richard Wagners (1826–1859)," *Die Königl. Sächs. musikalische Kapelle von Reissiger bis Schuch.* . . . Dresden: C. C. Meinhold & Söhne, 1898 9–40 (instrumentation).

1076 Voppel, Konrad. "Karl Straube und das Wesen des deutschen Orgelspiels," MuK XXV (1955) 90–96 (articulation in Bach).

W

1076.01 Wagner, Ernst. "Die alte Trompete in neuer Zeit," MWb XV (1884) 481–83, 497–99, 509–11 (instrumentation, J. S. Bach, Berlioz).

1077 ———. *Musikalische Ornamentik.* Berlin: [R. Lienau], 1869.

1078 Walker, Ernest. "The Appoggiatura," ML V (1924) 121–44 (esp. Bach, Mozart, Schubert).

1079 Wallner, Bertha Antonia. "Ein Instrumentenverzeichnis aus dem 16. Jahrhundert," Festschrift SANDBERGER 275–86 (quotes Praetorius, *et. al.*).

1080 Waltershausen, Hermann W. V. "Zur Aufführungspraxis der Musik Johann Sebastian Bachs," Mk XXII (1929–30) 256–61.

1080.01 Walther, Johann Gottfried. *Praecepta der Musicalischen Composition.* Weimar Landesbibliothek Signatur Hs Q 341c, 1708. NA ed. by P. Benary. Leipzig: Breitkopf & Härtel, 1955 (incl. ornamentation, rhythm, lexicon).

1081 Wangermée, Robert. "L'Improvisation pianistique au debut du XIXᵉ siècle," *Miscellanea Musicologica: Floris van der Mueren.* Ghent: [L. van Melle], 1950 227–53 (incl. preludes, cadenzas; quotes Mozart, Beethoven, Czerny, Chopin, *et al.*).

1082 ———. "Le traité du chant sur le livre de P. L. Pollio, maître de musique à la Collégiale Saint-Vincent à Soignies dans la seconde moitié du XVIIIᵉ siècle," *Hommage à Charles van den Borren: Mélanges*, ed. by M. Nijhoff. Antwerp: N. V. de Nederlandsche Boekhandel, 1945 336–50.

1083 Warner, Sylvia Townsend. "An Aspect of Tudor Counterpoint," ML II (1921) 35–49 (rhythm).

1084 Warner, Thomas E. "Indications of Performance Practice in Woodwind Instruction Books of the Seventeenth and Eighteenth Centuries," unpublished Ph.D. diss., New York University, 1964 (incl. articulation, tempo, ornaments, rhythm, improvisation, bibliography).

1085 Wasielewski, Wilhelm Joseph von. "Ein französischer Musikbericht aus der ersten Hälfte des 17. Jahrhunderts," MfM X (1878) 1–9, 17–23 (instrumental and vocal music in Rome; singing, orchestration, conducting).

1086 Weaver, Robert L. "Sixteenth-Century Instrumentation," MQ XLVII (1961) 363–78.

1087 Webbe, Samuel. *Harmony Epitomised.* . . . London: W. Hodsoll, [ca. 1810] (*b. c.*).

1088 Weber, Gottfried. "Einiges über die Einfache und die Doppelzunge und überhaupt über Articulation auf Blasinstrumenten insbesondere auf der Flöte," *Caecilia* IX (1828) 99–120.

1089 Weczerza, Walter. "Das koloristischinstrumentale Moment in den Symphonien Josef Haydns," unpublished Ph.D. diss., Vienna, 1923 (texture).

1090 Weidmann, Gudrun. "Die Violintechnik Paganinis," unpublished Ph.D. diss., Berlin, 1950.

1091 Weiermann, Herbert. "Der süddeutsche Orgelprospekt des 17. und 18. Jahrhunderts," unpublished Ph.D. diss., Munich, 1956.

1092 Wellesz, Egon. "Die Aussetzung des Basso Continuo in der italienischen Oper," KONGRESS 1911 (London) 282–85.

1093 ———. "Bemerkungen zur Musikpraxis um 1600," ZIMG XV (1913–1914) 133–35 (instrumental and vocal make-up).

1094 Welter, Friedrich Wilhelm. "Spiel und Kompositionen zu mehreren Orgeln vom 16. bis 19. Jahrhundert, vornehmlich in Oberitalien," unpublished Ph.D. diss., Berlin, 1923.

1094.01 Werba, Erik. "Das Mozart-Lied in der Aufführungspraxis der Gegenwart," Österr. MZ XXII (1967) 452–56.

1095 Werckmeister, Andreas. *Harmonologia musica, oder Kurtze Anleitung zur musikalischen Composition.* Frankfurt and Leipzig: Calvisius, 1702 (*b. c.*).

1096 ———. *Die nothwendigsten Anmerckungen, und Regeln wie der Bassus Continuus, oder General-Bass wohl könne tractiret werden . . .*, 2nd ed. Aschersleben: G. E. Struntz, 1715.

99

1097 Werra, Ernst von. "Beiträge zur Geschichte des französischen Orgel-spiels," KmJb XXIII (1910) 37–58 (16th–17th centuries).

1098 ——. "Beiträge zur Geschichte des katholischen Orgelspiels," KmJb XII (1897) 28–36.

1099 Westphal, Kurt. "Mit oder ohne Verzierungen?" *Das Musikleben* VI (1953) 41–43 (opera).

1100 Westrup, Jack Allan. "The Continuo in the 'St. Matthew Passion,'" Bachgedenkschrift 103–17.

1100.01 ——. "Monteverdi's 'Lamento d'Arianna,'" MR I (1940) 144–54 (text, *b. c.*, tempo).

1100.02 ——. "Monteverdi and the Orchestra," ML XXI (1940) 230–45.

1100.03 Weyman, Wesley. "The Passing of the Pressure Touch," MQ VII (1921) 127–32 (late 19th-century piano technique).

1100.031 White, E. Chappell. "Giovanni Baptista Viotti and his Violin Con-certos," unpublished Ph.D. diss., Princeton University, 1957 (incl. contemporary reports of Viotti's performances).

1100.032 Whittaker, William Gillies. "The Art of Accompaniment From Thorough-Bass," MT LXXIII (1932) 32–34, 123–25.

1100.04 ——. "Notes on Bach's Orchestration," *The Consort* No. 1 (1929) 1–4 (esp. number of players).

1101 Widor, Charles Marie and Albert Schweitzer. "Wie sind J. S. Bachs Präludien und Fugen auf unseren modernen Orgeln zu regis-trieren?" Mk X/1 (1910–11) 67–80, 143–57.

1101.01 Wieck, Friedrich. *Clavier und Gesang.* 2nd ed. Leipzig: Verlag von F. E. C. Leuckart, 1875. Eng. trans. for Mme. Clara Schumann and Miss Marie Wieck by H. Krueger as *Piano and Singing Didactical and Polemical: For Professionals and Amateurs.* Aber-deen: H. Krueger, 1875 (comprehensive; esp. valuable for knowledge of Clara Schumann).

1101.02 Wiedeburg, Michael Johann Friedrich. *Musikalisches Charten-Spiel ex g dur.* . . . Zurich: bey A. F. Winter, 1788 (extemporization).

1102 ——. *Der sich selbst informirende Clavierspieler.* . . . Halle and Leipzig: Verlag der Buchhandlung des Waisenhauses, 1765–75 (incl. *b. c.*).

1103 Williams, Charles Francis Abdy. "Concerning Performance," *Bach.* New York: Dutton, 1900 156–72 (temperament, ornamentation, fingering, *b. c.*).

1103.001 Williams, Sarah Jane. "Vocal Scoring in the Chansons of Machaut," JAMS XXI (1968) 251–57.

1103.01 Wilson, Steuart. "The Recitatives of the St. Matthew Passion," ML XVI (1935) 208–25 (incl. *b. c.*, rhythm, appoggiaturas).

1103.02 Winter, Paul. *Der mehrchörige Stil.* Frankfurt: C. F. Peters, 1964.

1104 Winternitz, Emanuel. *Musical Instruments and Their Symbolism in Western*

Art. New York: W. W. Norton, [1967] (incl. ensemble, instrumental playing).

1105 ——. "On Angel Concerts in the 15th Century: A Critical Approach to Realism and Symbolism in Sacred Painting," MQ XLIX (1963) 450–63 (incl. ensemble).

1106 Wintersgill, H. H. "Handel's Two-length Bar," ML XVII (1936) 1–12 (meter, rhythm, accents).

1107 Wlach, Hans. "Die Oboe bei Beethoven," StMw XIV (1927) 107–24.

1108 Wohlmuth, Hans. "Die Grundsätze deutscher Gesangskultur von 1750 bis 1790," unpublished Ph.D. diss., Vienna, 1924.

1109 Wohnhaas, Theodor. "Studien zur musikalischen Interpretationsfrage. (Anhand [*sic*] von Schallplattenaufnahmen der Coriolan-Ouvertüre Beethovens)," unpublished Ph.D. diss., Bonn, 1959.

1110 Wolf, Georg Friedrich. *Kurzer Unterricht im Clavierspielen.* Göttingen: 1783.

1111 ——. *Unterricht im Klavierspielen*, 2 vols. in 1. Halle: Johann Christian Hendel, 1789 (incl. fingering, ornamentation, *b. c.*).

1112 ——. *Unterricht in der Singekunst.* Halle: Johann Christian Hendel, 1784.

1113 Wolf, Hans. "Die musikalischen Bewegungsbegriffe in den Generalbass- und Kompositionslehren des 18. Jahrhunderts als Fortsetzung der Lehre vom Kontrapunkt," unpublished Ph.D. diss., Vienna, 1936.

1114 Wolf, Robert Erich. "T⁻e Aesthetic Problem of the Renaissance," RB IX (1955) 83–102 (expression).

1115 Wolff, Hellmuth Christian. "Gesangs-Improvisationen der Barockzeit," *Das Musikleben* VI (1953) 46–49 (quotes Bacilly).

1116 ——. "Die Gesangsimprovisationen der Barockzeit," KONGRESS 1953 (Bamberg) 252–55.

1116.01 ——. "Moderne Aufführungspraxis der Barockoper," *Das Musikleben* V (1952) 169–72.

1117 ——. "Die Musik im alten Venedig," *Festschrift Heinrich Besseler zum sechzigsten Geburtstag*, ed. by Institut für Musikwissenschaft der Karl-Marx-Universität. Leipzig: VEB Deutscher Verlag für Musik 1961 291–303 (instruments).

1117.01 Wolgast, Gesa (ed.). Prefaces to Georg Böhm's *Sämtliche Werke*, Vol. I. Wiesbaden: Breitkopf & Härtel, [1952] (quotes ornamentation tables, organ stop lists).

1118 Wollitz, Kenneth. "An Introduction to Baroque Ornamentation," AR VII/1 (1966) 4–10.

1118.01 Wood, Ralph W. "Putting in the Expression," ML XI (1930) 375–82 (dynamics).

1119 Woodcock, Edith (ed.). Preface to Baldassare Galuppi's *Six Sonatas for Keyboard Instruments.* New York: Galaxy Music, 1963 (incl. ornaments).

101

1120 Wright, Daniel. *The Compleat Tutor for ye Flute.* . . . London: for the
author, [ca. 1735] (recorder).

1121 Wustmann, Rudolf. "Vom Rhythmus des evangelischen Chorals," BJ
VII (1910) 86–102.

Y

1122 Young, Percy Marshall. *Messiah: A Study in Interpretation.* London: D.
Dobson, [1951].

Z

1123 [Zacconi, Lodovico]. "Die Gorgia. Über die Ausführung der Kolora-
turen und den Gebrauch der modernen Passagen," VfMw
VII (1891) 341–96.

1124 ——. *Prattica di musica* . . ., 2 pts. Venice: Bartolomeo Carampello,
1596, and Venice: Alessandro Vincenti, 1622.

1125 Zarlino, Gioseffo. *Le Istitvtioni harmoniche* . . .. Venice: [n. p.], 1558.

1126 Zavarský, Ernest. "Zum Pedalspiel des jungen Johann Sebastian
Bach," Mf XVIII (1965) 370–78.

1127 Zeller, Bernhard. "Das Recitativo accompagnato in den Opern
Johann Adolf Hasses," unpublished Ph.D. diss., Halle, 1911
(*b. c.*).

1128 Zingel, Hans Joachim. "Studien zur Geschichte des Harfenspiels in
klassischer und romantischer Zeit," AfMf II (1937) 455–65.

1129 Zschinsky-Troxler, Elsa Margherita von. "Das violintechnik Problem,"
Gaetano Pugnani. Berlin: Atlantis, 1939 217–27 (phrasing, tone,
vibrato, bowing).

1130 [Zumbag de Koesfelt, Coenraad]. *Institutiones musicae.* . . . Leiden:
G. Potvliet, 1743 (*b. c.*).

1131 Zuth, Josef. "Instrumentaltechnik," *Simon Molitor und die Wiener
Gitarristik* (*um 1800*). Vienna: Goll, 1919 40–61 (fingering).

index

Since the authors appear alphabetically in the main Bibliography, they have not been listed again in the following Index. Thus, in order to find all of the literature for a given historical figure, one must look for his name in both the main Bibliography and the Index.

A

accentuation, vocal music, 552.01
Agazarri, A., 877.01
Albert, H., 291
Albrechtsberger, J. G., 1037
Allegri, G., 32
Amat, J. C., 831
Ammerbach, N., 55.02
Anglican chant, 845.01
anthem, T. Tomkins, 180.01
appoggiatura, F. Schubert, 42.01, 817.01
Arbeau, T., 76.01
Ariosi, A., 141
articulation, 263, 532, 533, 584, 816.001, 1016.02; Renaissance, 865; 16th century, 493; 17th century, 493, 622; 18th century, 253.01, 372, 480, 527, 555, 846.01, 1014; 19th century, 441.01; cornett, 846; flageolet, 405.01; flute, 205, 255.01, 255.02, 643.01; 769.02, 1088; harpsichord, 432; keyboard, 574, 1034; lute, 602, 758; oboe, 310; organ, 536, 845, 1016; recorder, 256.02, 344.01, 495; trumpet, 27, 28, 954; violin, 146, 147, 370, 888; vocal, 94, 379, 552.01, 845.02, 887; woodwinds, 1084; J. S. Bach, 348.01, 532, 550, 557, 561, 570, 611, 771.01, 772, 827, 860, 882, 964, 982, 1052, 1076; L. v. Beethoven, 241.01, 348.01, 780, 885; J. Brahms, 707; D. Buxtehude, 502; F. Chopin, 456; F. Couperin, 679; C. Gounod, 348.01; G. F. Handel, 348.01, 1106; F. J. Haydn, 607; W. A. Mozart, 17.01, 307.01, 532, 542.01, 704, 884, 885, 993; D. Scarlatti, 530; R. Schumann, 348.01; H. Schütz, 482
Aubert, J., 960

B

Bach, C. P. E., 294, 342, 460, 612, 828, 860.01, 1077; clavichord, 936; dynamics, 515, 516; fingering, 55.02; keyboard, 739, 995, 996, 1010; ornamentation, 907, 918
Bach, Johann Christian, 901
Bach, J. S., 227, 250, 300.01, 342, 390, 460, 626.02, 703.01, 762, 766.01, 828, 886, 946, 984, 994, 1012, 1080; articulation, 348.01, 532, 557, 561, 570, 771.01, 772, 982, 1076; choral music, 611, 680, 724, 735, 1035; dynamics, 112; fingering, 55.02, 56, 1103; harpsichord, 15, 603.01; instrumentation, 5, 111, 440, 501, 523, 545, 609, 660, 894, 1004, 1032, 1033, 1051.01, 1100.04; interpretation, 53; keyboard, 90, 116, 117, 158, 190.01, 260.01, 284, 286.02, 298.01, 309, 431, 464, 490, 531, 545, 584.01, 607.01, 609, 784, 785, 827, 940, 964, 1051.01, 1052; lute, 331; organ, 21, 23, 199.01, 259, 269, 300.02, 405.04, 532.01, 559, 560, 561, 562, 568, 583.01, 627.01, 801, 811, 906, 1076, 1101, 1126; ornamentation, 20, 21, 22.01, 23, 56, 242, 286.02, 299, 299.01, 300, 547, 584.01, 607.01, 629, 650, 682, 726, 727, 763, 764, 906, 924, 1078, 1103; recitative, 273, 677; repeats, 814; rhythm, 56, 268, 269, 300, 301, 301.01, 490, 491, 506, 585, 607.01, 675, 761.01, 764, 775, 799, 883, 924; stringed instruments, 354; tempo, 112, 269, 405.04, 535, 560, 561, 883, 1051.01; trumpet, 107, 287.01, 1076.01; tuning, 75, 681, 1103; tympani, 1031.04; vega bow,

58, 1005, 1029, 1030, 1031; violin music, 58, 121, 143, 146, 147, 594, 678, 951, 959, 1031, 1047; *Art of Fugue*, 500, 626.01; *Brandenburg Concerto No. 2*, 484; Cantatas, 276, 676, 767, 860, 933, 1072; *Chromatic Fantasy*, 650; *Goldberg Variations*, 200.01, 550; *Mass in B Minor*, 275, 282, 285; Motets, 161, 281, 472; *Musical Offering*, 249, 346.001, 803; Orchestral Suites, 82; Organ Preludes and Fugues, 300.02; Partitas, 298.01, 603.01; *St. John Passion*, 110, 488, 684, 687, 859, 1000; *St. Matthew Passion*, 83, 368.01, 488, 496.02, 509, 687, 1100, 1103.01; *Vor deinen Thron tret ich hiemit*, 780.01; *Well-tempered Clavier*, 457, 498.01, 882

Bach, W. F., 740

Bacilly, B. de, 179, 400, 1115

bagpipe, 17th century, 122.03; 18th century, 493.01

basse dance, 226.02, 446, 448

basso continuo, 1.01, 226.01, 667, 781, 792.01, 862.02, 930, 943, 1003, 1100.032; 17th century, 12, 46, 103, 105, 122, 152, 191, 267, 283, 289, 291, 364.01, 365, 366, 432, 534, 547, 583, 612, 622, 628, 685, 714, 747, 757, 773, 777, 787, 797.02, 804, 824.02, 851, 878, 879, 899, 902, 914, 967, 981, 988, 1042, 1044, 1046, 1067, 1068, 1069, 1092, 1095, 1096, 1100.01, 1127; 18th century, 1.02, 8, 13, 18, 18.01, 26, 33, 43, 46, 60, 61, 66, 69, 77, 86, 92, 93, 93.01, 95, 98, 109, 122.02, 124, 129, 135, 159, 159.01, 162, 197, 213, 215, 238, 244, 248, 252, 312, 320, 324, 325, 326.01, 338, 345, 353, 365, 369, 371, 382, 405, 408, 416, 417, 432, 436, 451, 452, 452.01, 455, 467.01, 471, 472, 486, 504, 529, 534, 536.01, 537, 538, 541, 551, 552, 577, 598, 604, 612, 613, 614, 617, 619, 631, 649, 656, 665, 669, 670, 671, 676, 684, 708, 710, 715.01, 728, 733, 734, 756, 774, 782, 783, 784, 785, 792, 795, 818, 821, 822, 823.01, 825, 834, 840, 841, 850, 858, 860, 863, 870, 874, 889, 896, 902, 944, 946, 952, 972, 975, 978, 979, 984, 994, 1026, 1028, 1037, 1038, 1042, 1048, 1050, 1054, 1092, 1100, 1102, 1103, 1103.01, 1111, 1113, 1127, 1130; 19th century, 91, 164, 227, 231, 272, 443, 564, 566, 733, 821, 1087

bassoon, comprehensive, 790

Beethoven, L. v., 55.01, 497, 595, 626.02, 780, 1081; articulation 241.01, 348.01, 885; dynamics, 474, 885; instrumentation, 438.01, 1107; ornamentation, 149, 241.01, 286.01, 434.01, 804.01; piano, 232, 286.01, 358.02, 661.02, 662, 717, 864.02, 904.01, 974; repeats, 468, 469, 470; rhythm, 855, 885; tempo, 85, 87, 251, 576, 717, 989, 1062; *Coriolan Overture*, 1109; *Fidelio*, 221; *Missa Solemnis*, 644; Opus 96, 512; *Symphony No. 3*, 625, 977.01; *Symphony No. 5*, 352, 977.01; *Violin Concerto*, 1053.01

Beissel, J. C., 106.01

bel canto, see monody; opera; voice, comprehensive

Berard, J.-A., 750

Berlioz, H., trumpet, 1076.01

Bermudo, J., 1009

Bernhard, C., 740.01

Besard, J.-B. 1016.01

Biber, H., 1, 7, 638

Blow, J., 39, 40

Bovicelli, B., 400

bowed instruments, 806, 871

bowing, 266, 823.01; *see also* violin, bowing; violoncello, bowing

Brahms, J., 321, 322, 626.02, 706, 707

brass instruments, 311, 991, 1063

Brossard, S., 675

Brumel, A., 173

Burmeister, J., 895

Buxtehude, D., 502.01, 583, 583.01, 673

Byrd, W., 32.01, 90

C

Cabanilles, J., 1065

Cabezón, A. de, 868.01

Caccini, G., 166, 167, 168

cadenza, 18th century, 921, 923; piano, 567, 1011, 1049, 1081; violin, 810; W. A. Mozart, 711.01

Campian, T., 323

Carissimi, G., 173.001, 227, 289, 877.02

castrati, 140, 414, 465

Cavalieri, E., 180, 227

cembalo, *see* harpsichord, keyboard

Charpentier, M. A., 479.01

Chopin, F., 477.04, 485, 554.01, 1081; articulation, 456; dynamics, 189, 456; ornamentation, 279.02, 789; tempo, 189, 456, 521, 608, 857, 966.01; Opus 10, 172

choral music, Baroque, 796.01; 16th century, 1103.02; 17th century, 32.003, 1103.02; 19th century, 827.01; sacred, 13.01, 32.003, 908.02; *see also* vocal music

church music, 239, 240, 697, 1056; 15th century, 925.01; 16th century, 95.01, 150.01, 620.01, 664.01, 1008.01; 17th century, 32.003, 965.04; vocal music, 13.01, 32.003, 908.02; *see also* individual composers; instrumentation, vocal music

clarinet, 188, 229, 826, 886.01

clavichord, 434, 769, 898, 944.01; C. P. E. Bach, 936; *see also* keyboard

clavichord-harpsichord-piano question, 50, 115, 153, 158, 228, 284, 406.01, 426, 431, 498.01, 759, 793.01; *see also* instrumentation

clavier, *see* clavichord, harpsichord, keyboard, piano

comprehensive, 114, 245, 248.01, 254, 263.01, 265, 270, 355, 412, 428, 438, 454, 481, 489, 508.01, 691, 692, 701.01, 761, 919, 965.05, 969.01, 1013, 1017, 1020.01, 1041.01; Medieval, 1059; Renaissance, 160.01; Baroque, 19, 128, 170, 766, 947.001; 14th century, 17, 813; 15th century, 335, 813, 1039, 1125; 16th century, 134, 185, 200, 335, 374, 388, 716, 1124, 1125; 17th century, 184, 185, 190, 247, 263, 264, 350.01, 374, 388, 558, 600.01, 624.01, 639, 688, 703, 777, 779, 808, 820, 968, 1019, 1080.01, 1085; 18th century, 84.01, 192, 247, 263, 266, 460, 505, 555, 590.01, 610, 635.001, 646, 655, 657, 672, 689, 715.01, 753.01, 779, 802, 808, 856, 909, 914.01, 977, 980, 1019, 1022, 1031.02, 1032.01, 1032.02, 1048, 1080.01

concerto grosso, instrumentation, 508.02

conducting, 174, 196, 410, 487, 518.01, 953, 955, 1036, 1070; Medieval, 542; Baroque, 358.01; 16th century, 195, 196; 17th century, 195, 290, 895, 956, 1085; 18th century, 175, 195, 199, 359, 956; 19th century, 359, 367; orchestra, 358.01

Conti, F., 355.02

continuo, *see basso continuo*

contratanz, 994.01

Corelli, A., 213, 252, 347, 1023; ornamentation, 806.01; Opus 5, 212, 720, 872; *Christmas Concerto*, 511

cornett, 846

Corrette, M., 477.01

Corri, D., 862.02

Costeley, G., 222

countering, 673.01

countertenor, 910.01

Couperin, F., 55.02, 225, 678.01, 679, 796

Czerny, C., 884, 974, 1081

D

dance music, 47, 76.01, 198, 401.01, 448, 510.01, 558, 674.01; *see also* basse dance

declamation, 276.01; trouvères, 1062.02

Demantius, C., 119
diminution, *see* ornamentation
Diruta, G., 583.02
Dowland, J., 227, 753
Dowland, R., 753
Dubourg, M., 806.01
Dufay, G., 990, 1060
Durante, F., 638.01
dynamics, 297, 430, 584, 1118.01; Renaissance, 119, 587, 623; 17th century, 142, 290,
    1018, 1019; 18th century, 142, 370, 372, 473, 475, 480, 867, 1014, 1018, 1019;
    C. P. E. Bach, 515, 516; J. S. Bach, 112, 147, 464, 550, 611, 684, 801, 860, 964,
    1000; W. F. Bach, 740; L. v. Beethoven, 474, 780, 885; J. Brahms, 321, 707; M. A.
    Charpentier, 479.01; F. Chopin, 189, 456; L. Janáček, 1071; J. C. Kerll, 384.01;
    W. A. Mozart, 255, 305, 473, 652.01, 993; G. Muffat, 746; M. Reger, 616; F.
    Schubert, 148

E

editing, 1008
embellishment, *see* ornamentation
ensembles, *see* instrumentation; orchestras, composition of
equestrian ballet, 1040
expression, 615; Renaissance, 1114; 17th century, 444; 18th century, 52, 253.01, 444;
    19th century, 441.01; C. Monteverdi, 788.01; *see also* comprehensive

F

Farrant, R., 227
fermatas, *see* rhythm, tempo
figurate descant, 968
figured bass, *see* basso continuo
Filtz, A., 867
Finck, H., 292, 546
fingering, clarinet, 886.01; flageolet, 104.02, 405.01; harpsichord, 432, 436, 794;
    keyboard, 449, 554, 653, 734, 816, 1111; organ, 536, 845; piano, 2, 4, 733, 1049;
    recorder, 344.01; N. Ammerbach, 55.02; C. P. E. Bach, 55.02; J. S. Bach, 55.02,
    550, 1103; D. Buxtehude, 502.01; F. Couperin, 55.02; C. Merulo, 509.01; W. A.
    Mozart, 731; H. Purcell, 833; J. J. Quantz, 55.02; T. de Santa Maria, 55.02
Fitzwilliam Virginal Book, 333, 358, 955.02
flageolet, 17th century, 350.01, 405.01; 18th century, 104.01, 769.01; articulation,
    405.01; fingering, 104.01, 405.01; ornamentation, 104.01
flute, 94.01, 371, 677.01, 942; comprehensive, 205, 216, 360, 439, 494, 635.01, 732,
    822.01, 823, 835, 941; 17th century, 350.01; 18th century, 255.01, 255.02, 256.02,
    411.01, 643.01, 769.02, 1047.01; articulation, 255.01, 255.02, 1088; ornamentation,
    255.01, 255.02
Frescobaldi, G., 351, 1064.01
frottole, 812
Fux, J. J., 916

G

Gabrieli, G., 45, 596, 792.01
Gagliano, M. de, 383.02
Galilei, V., 314
Galuppi, B., 1119
Ganassi, S., 120

106

Gasparini, G., 612, 878
Geminiani, F., 55, 120, 142.01, 145.01, 213, 243, 612
general bass, *see basso continuo*
Gibbons, O., 227
Gluck, C. W., 227, 390; opera, 893; ornamentation, 917; recitatives, 944; rhythm, 702; *Orfeo*, 336
Gounod, C., articulation, 348.01
Görner, J. V., 581
Graun, C. H., 252
Graviseth, J. von, 190
Grétry, A.-M., 836
Grocheo, J., 293
guitar, comprehensive, 177, 447, 831; 17th century, 32.001, 749.01; fingering, 113; tuning, 187.02

H

Hammerschmidt, A., 424, 622
Handel, G. F., 163, 213, 227, 244, 390, 394, 540, 578, 786, 828; articulation, 348.01, 1106; instrumentation, 108, 188, 315, 319, 478, 1074; keyboard, 90, 940; opera, 344, 652, 892, 912; oratorio, 668; organ, 503; ornamentation, 401, 404, 421, 668, 1073; rhythm, 404, 775, 1106; tempo, 404, 409; trumpet, 287.01; *Messiah*, 100, 193, 462, 963, 965.02, 1122; *O Come, Let Us Sing*, 796.01; *St. John Passion*, 13
harp, 18th century, 576.01
harpsichord, 371, 395, 427, 436.01, 822.01, 823, 944.01; comprehensive, 15, 92, 93, 223, 312, 432, 450, 633, 817, 898, 903, 913, 1110; 18th century, 5.01, 576.01; fingering, 93, 436, 794; ornamentation, 34, 337, 436, 442, 593, 633, 794; registration, 603.01; tuning, 436, 794; J. S. Bach, 15, 603.01; F. Couperin, 678.01; *see also* clavichord-harpsichord-piano question, keyboard
Hasse, J. A., 519, 1127
Havingha, G., 442
Haydn, F. J., 227, 406.01; keyboard, 51; ornamentation, 935; orchestra, 498.02; piano, 793.01; rhythm, 855; Symphonies, 607, 1089
Heinichen, J. D., 159.01
horn, 709
Hummel, J. N., 149, 499.01
hurdy gurdy, 1031.03; 18th century, 213.02, 279.03

I

improvisation, 88, 184, 327, 328, 329, 330; 15th century, 816, 890; 16th century, 911; 18th century, 405.02, 576.01, 923, 972.01, 977.02, 1069.01, 1101.02; 19th century, 499.01; *basso continuo* as, 269.01; harp, 576.01; harpsichord, 576.01; keyboard, 61, 405.02, 527, 1069.01; orchestral, 877.01; organ, 340, 553, 569, 844, 957; piano, 229.02; viola da gamba, 788; vocal, 220, 429, 463, 712, 741, 751, 816.01, 887, 1045, 1082, 1115, 1116; woodwinds ,1084; W. A. Mozart, 512.01; *see also* ornamentation, individual instruments, comprehensive, *basso continuo*
instrumentation, 173.01, 174, 263.02, 584, 693, 694; Medieval, 137, 138, 139, 139.01, 150, 160, 186, 187, 256, 293, 295, 350, 361, 373, 383, 387, 401.01, 425, 437, 675.01, 696, 768, 816.01, 847, 905, 920, 986, 1104; Renaissance, 150, 280.01, 361, 695, 768, 812, 986, 1104; Baroque, 226.01, 358.01, 522, 524, 930; 15th century, 621, 624, 736, 816.01, 927, 990, 1105; 16th century, 14, 44.01, 88, 198, 286, 296, 304, 556, 635, 722, 778, 854, 945, 961, 1079, 1086, 1117; 17th century, 10, 149.01, 154, 175.01, 184, 190, 196.02, 279.01, 290, 347, 383.01, 383.02, 385, 396, 399, 476.01, 526, 597, 605, 674.01, 760, 945, 973, 1019, 1040, 1043, 1085, 1093, 1117; 18th century,

131, 133, 175, 182, 229, 254.01, 385, 476.01, 826, 1019, 1117, 1128; 19th century, 827.01, 1075, 1117, 1128; church music, 44.01, 123, 286, 402, 483, 556, 596, 836, 842, 877, 965.04, 1014; *concerto grosso*, 508.02; dance music, 47; J. S. Bach, 5, 111, 249, 440, 500, 501, 523, 545, 609, 611, 660, 626.01, 684, 687, 735, 767, 803, 860, 894, 933, 1004, 1032, 1033, 1035, 1072, 1100.04; L. v. Beethoven, 438.01, 1107; G. Carissimi, 877.02; M. A. Charpentier, 479.01; G. Gabrieli, 45; G. F. Handel, 108, 188, 193, 315, 319, 478, 1074; F. J. Haydn, 607; O. Lassus, 349, 1058; G. de Machaut, 848, 849; C. Monteverdi, 122.01, 145, 384, 389, 787, 1100.02; W. A. Mozart, 68, 84, 234, 255, 303, 305, 966; G. Muffat, 743, 746; M. Mussorgsky, 171.01; P. Ritter, 295.01; H. Schütz, 685, 686, 875; G. P. Telemann, 701, 1027; A. Vivaldi, 700; R. Wagner, 407
instruments, 445, 493, 688, 820, 968

J

Janáček, L., 1071
Jobardini, B., 525
Jullien, G., 513
justiniane, 890

K

Kerll, J. C., 384.01
kettledrums, J. S. Bach, 1031.04
keyboard, 56, 61, 332, 929, 944.01, 961.01; comprehensive, 8, 61, 93.01, 96, 133.01, 415, 544, 554, 564, 565, 598, 631, 653, 658, 734, 816, 832, 870, 1102, 1111; Renaissance, 508; Baroque, 401.001, 542.001; 15th century, 389.01; 16th century, 32.002, 790.02, 869; 17th century, 7.01, 187.01, 525, 723.01, 747.01, 864.01, 869, 955.02; 18th century, 5.01, 254.01, 256.01, 317.01, 405.02, 467.01, 635.001, 663, 715.01, 864.01, 869, 940, 977.02, 1069.01; 19th century, 317.01; articulation, 574, 1034; fingering, 289, 449, 565, 574; improvisation, 61; ornamentation, 61, 90, 93.01, 157, 187.01, 256.01, 317.01, 401.001, 554.02, 565, 584.01, 723.01, 747.01, 790.02, 864.01; rhythm, 542.001; tempo, 7.01; texture, 635.02; C. P. E. Bach, 739; J. S. Bach, 56, 90, 116, 117, 158, 190.01, 260.01, 284, 286.02, 490, 531, 584.01, 603.01, 607.01, 609, 784, 785, 940; W. Byrd, 90; G. F. Handel, 90, 940; J. Kuhnau, 723.01, 791; C. Merulo, 509.01; W. A. Mozart, 65, 153, 156, 512.01, 542.01, 731, 864; T. Muffat, 864.01; H. Purcell, 90; J. P. Sweelinck, 229.01; *see also* clavichord, harpsichord, organ, piano
Kirnberger, J. P., 252, 460
klavier, *see* clavichord, harpsichord, keyboard, organ, piano
Kraus, J. M., 307
Kuhnau, J., 593, 723.01, 791

L

Landini, F., 295
Lassus, O., 349, 1058
Lalande, M.-R. de, 182, 183
Leclair, J.-M., violin, 626, 823.01, 823.02
lira da braccio, 258, 405.03
Liszt, F., 358.02, 393, 396, 458, 606
liturgical drama, 973.01
Loeillet, J.-B., 633
Lorenzoni, A., 360

108

Louis XIV, 149.01, 1040
Ludford, N., 95.01
Lully, J.-B., 210, 601, 807, 960
lute, 323, 908; comprehensive, 77, 118, 178, 246, 639, 753, 758, 1016.01; 16th
century, 271.002; 17th century, 279.01, 479.02; fingering, 571, 572; ornamenta-
tion, 246, 260, 368, 575, 602; scordatura, 602; tuning, 271.002, 572, 575; J. S.
Bach, 331
Luther, M., 227
Luzzaschi, L., 837

M

Machaut, G. de, 187, 373, 848, 849, 1103.001
madrigal, 277, 278, 538.01, 674, 879; see also vocal music, 16th century
madrigal comedy, 72
Malvezzi, C., 647
mandolin, 479.03
Manfredini, V., 712
Mannheim School, 476.001
Marcello, B., 797
Marenzio, L., 277
Marini, B., 1, 120
Marpurg, F. W., 460, 834, 884, 1077
Matteis, N., 364.01
Mattheson, J., 850
Mazzochi, D., 674
Mendelssohn, F., 1061
Merulo, C., 509.01
Michael, T., 10
Milton, J., 41, 150.01
Molitor, S., 1131
Mondonville, J.-J. C., 809
monody, 25, 34.01, 166, 167, 168, 180, 280, 314, 406, 792.002, 792.01, 798, 837, 970,
976, 1043
Montéclair, M. P., 131
Monteverdi, C., 737, 851, 1127; expression, 788.01; instrumentation, 145, 384,
1100.02; orchestra, 43.01; ornamentation, 1007; L'Incoronazione di Poppea, 43.01,
852; Lagrime d'Amante al Sepolcro dell'Amate, 796.01; Lamento d'Arianna, 1100.01;
Madrigali Guerrieri . . ., 714; Orfeo, 787, 830, 852; Scherzi Musicali . . ., 715;
Vespers, 122.01, 389, 852
Morales, C. de, 627
Moravian music, 104.01
Moscheles, I., 974
Mozart, L., 55, 339, 376, 377, 775
Mozart, W. A., 341, 342, 390, 729, 828, 1081; accentuation, 55.01; articulation,
17.01, 55.01, 307.01, 532, 704, 885; bowing, 677.02; dynamics, 255, 305, 473,
652.01, 885; fingering, 55.02, 731; improvisation, 512.01; instrumentation, 55.01,
68, 84, 234, 303, 305; keyboard, 65, 153, 156, 307.01, 476.002, 512.01, 542.01, 731,
864, 884; orchestra, 643.02; organ, 542.01; ornamentation, 64, 65, 305, 901, 971,
992, 1016.03, 1078; piano, 346.01, 897.01; rhythm, 855, 885; tempo, 55.01, 67,
298, 381, 742, 838, 998, 999; tone production, 55.01; trumpet, 287.01; violin, 738;
vocal music, 1094.01; Don Giovanni, 381; Idomeneo, 966; Piano Concertos, 476.002;
Symphony No. 41, 993; Violin Sonatas, 652.01; Die Zauberflöte, 476, 966, 1074.01;
K.107, 711.01; K.497, 542.02; K.521, 542.02; K.593, 542.02

Muffat, G., 210, 864.01, 916
Muffat, T., 864.01
musette, *see* bagpipe
Mussorgsky, M., instrumentation, 171.01; *Boris Godunov*, 171.01

N

Nicolai, G. F., 505.01
Niedt, F. E., 382
notes inégales, *see* rhythm, *notes inégales*

O

oboe, comprehensive, 310, 419, 494, 822.01, 823; 17th century, 350.01; timbre, 664
opera, 26.01, 169, 179.01, 181, 313, 317, 336, 344, 395, 396, 399, 404.01, 620, 651,
661, 792.002, 797, 839, 1002, 1053, 1092, 1099, 1116.01; *see also* monody
opéra comique, Baroque, 76.011
oratorio, 406, 519, 861; *see also* monody
orchestra, 618.01, 950; Baroque, 358.01; 19th century, 826.01, 827.01; improvisation,
877.01; F. J. Haydn, 498.02; C. Monteverdi, 43.01; W. A. Mozart, 643.02
orchestras, composition of, 74, 78, 97, 183, 279, 307, 413, 497, 600, 1093; *see also*
instrumentation
organ, 155.01, 343, 502, 544, 891, 929, 955.01, 1046, 1091; comprehensive, 8, 568,
825, 873, 910, 934, 947, 958, 1016, 1051, 1094, 1097, 1098; Renaissance, 922.01;
Baroque, 1015, 1069.02; 15th century, 797.01; 925.01; 17th century, 71.02, 149.001,
213.002, 260.02, 742.01, 777.001, 812.01, 1117.01; 18th century, 5.01, 102.01,
112.01, 355.01, 566.01, 583.01, 908.01, 908.03; 19th century, 635.03, 942.01;
articulation, 536, 583.01, 845; expression, 583.01; fingering, 536, 845; improvisation, 340, 553, 569, 844, 957; ornamentation, 257, 271.02, 496, 513, 742.01, 777.001,
812.01, 1021, 1069.02, 1117.01; pedal, 113, 199.01, 915; registration, 8, 112.01,
213.002, 255, 271, 300.02, 355.01, 368.02, 496, 563, 645, 777.001, 915, 931, 962,
1021, 1065, 1069.02, 1101; tempo, 405.04; tuning, 501.01, 539, 931; J. S. Bach, 21,
23, 199.01, 259, 269, 300.02, 405.04, 559, 560, 561, 562, 568, 627.01, 666, 801, 811,
906, 1101, 1126; G. Frescobaldi, 1064.01; G. F. Handel, 503; W. A. Mozart,
542.01; J. Pachelbel, 777.01
ornamentation, 99, 101, 233, 241, 302, 316, 348, 356.01, 357, 375, 422.01, 423, 497.02,
532.02, 599, 642, 765.01, 790.01, 873.01, 994.01, 1020, 1025, 1077; Medieval,
1033.01; Renaissance, 106, 492, 868, 1006, 1033.01; Baroque, 22, 24, 73, 102,
209.01, 356, 401.001, 698, 819, 1006, 1118, 1123; 16th century, 79, 80, 88, 136, 237,
493, 770, 876, 938; 17th century, 26.02, 44, 154.01, 184, 260, 262, 290, 311.01, 326,
493, 808, 824.02, 938, 965; 18th century, 26.02, 35, 36, 37, 125, 133, 237.01, 262,
266, 326, 372, 467.01, 480, 554.02, 582, 610, 637, 652.02, 655, 689, 808, 828, 834,
897.02, 918, 921, 926, 939, 972.01, 1016.04, 1071.01; 19th century, 441.01, 441.02,
897.02; bassoon, 790; clarinet, 886.01; flageolet, 104.01; flute, 205, 255.01, 255.02,
635.01, 643.01, 769.02; guitar, 177; harpsichord, 34, 337, 432, 436, 442, 593, 633,
794, 809; keyboard, 61, 90, 93.01, 157, 187.01, 256.01, 317.01, 358, 401.001,
467.01, 527, 554, 554.02, 565, 584.01, 631, 653, 734, 747.01, 790.02, 816, 832,
864.01, 870, 1111; lute, 246, 260, 368, 575, 602; oboe, 310; organ, 257, 271.02, 496,
742.01, 777.001, 812.01, 1021; piano, 2, 378.01, 733, 1049; recorder, 247.01,
256.02, 362, 905.01; viola da gamba, 788, 967; violin, 71, 144, 176, 210, 212, 370,
630, 888, 904, 1012, 1023; violoncello, 217; vocal 26.02, 62, 71.01, 94, 106.02, 151,
179, 194, 208, 209, 219, 220, 263.03, 274, 289, 292, 306, 379, 400, 435, 463, 492,
521.01, 521.02, 546, 591, 592, 632, 648, 654, 712, 751, 752, 824, 829, 845.02, 887,
928, 964.01, 1041, 1045, 1099; voice, 280.001, 316.01, 441.02, 824.01; woodwinds,

110

1084; C. P. E. Bach, 907, 918, 995, 996, 1103.01; Johann Christian Bach, 901;
J. S. Bach, 20, 21, 22.01, 23, 56, 286.02, 299, 299.01, 300, 543, 550, 584.01, 629,
650, 682, 726, 727, 763, 764, 827, 906, 924, 1012, 1052, 1078, 1103; A. Banchieri,
71.01; L. v. Beethoven, 149, 241.01, 286.01, 595, 793.01; J. Bermudo, 1009; J.
Blow, 40; G. Carissimi, 877.02; F. Chopin, 279.02, 789; A. Corelli, 720, 806.01;
F. Couperin, 223, 224, 225, 679, 796; J. J. Fux, 916; B. Galuppi, 1119; C. W.
Gluck, 917; G. F. Handel, 401, 421, 668, 963, 1073; F. J. Haydn, 935; J. N.
Hummel, 149; J. Kuhnau, 791; J.-M. Leclair, 823.01, 823.02; J.-B. Lully, 807;
L. Luzzaschi, 837; C. Merulo, 509.01; C. Monteverdi, 830, 1007; W. A. Mozart,
64, 65, 305, 542.02, 901, 971, 992, 1016.03, 1078; G. Muffat, 745, 916; T. Muffat,
748, 749; G. Palestrina, 422; H. Purcell, 104, 267, 832, 833, 1064; J.-P. Rameau,
796; G. Rossini, 181.01; D. Scarlatti, 530, 549; F. Schubert, 42.01, 817.01, 1078;
G. Tartini, 271.001; R. Wagner, 960.01
Ortiz, D., 853

P

Pachelbel, J., 777.01
Paganini, N., 1, 200.001, 1090, 1129
Palestrina, G., 49, 422, 510
Peri, J., 798
Petri, S., 113
piano, comprehensive, 2, 3, 230, 346, 499, 518, 733, 793, 1100.03, 1049; 18th century,
5.01; 19th century, 197.01, 220.01, 229.02, 378.01, 775.01, 798.01, 1101.01;
articulation, 4; cadenzas, 567, 1011, 1081; fingering, 2, 4; improvisation, 229.02;
ornamentation, 2, 286.01, 378.01, 733; pedal, 2, 4, 775.01, 1101.01; rhythm,
798.01; J. S. Bach, 309, 964; L. v. Beethoven, 232, 286.01, 358.02, 661.02, 662, 717,
864.02, 904.01, 974; F. Chopin, 172; F. J. Haydn, 793.01; F. Liszt, 358.02, 386,
606; W. A. Mozart, 307.01, 346.01, 476.002, 897.01, 997; F. Schubert, 1020.02;
R. Schumann, 117.01, 250.01
piano concerto, W. A. Mozart, 476.002
Playford, J. 982.02
Pollio, P.-L., 1082
Praetorius, M., 1, 119, 290, 605, 1055, 1079
Prelleur, P., 145.01
pronunciation, 17th century, 947.01
Purcell, H., 833, 877.001, 987, 1064; fingering, 833; keyboard, 90, 832; ornamenta-
tion, 833; rhythm, 267; tempo, 833; vocal music, 104, 152; *Bell Anthem*, 965.03;
Orpheus Brittanicus, 42

Q

Quantz, J. J., 55, 55.02, 192, 268, 294, 762, 775, 834, 846.01, 884

R

Rameau, J.-P., 796, 842
Rebel, J.-F., 131
recitative, 211, 271.01, 379, 406.001, 428.01, 861; J. S. Bach, 273, 677, 684, 1035;
C. W. Gluck, 702, 944; G. F. Handel, 13; H. Schütz, 685; G. P. Telemann, 701,
1027
recorder, comprehensive, 494, 969, 1120; 17th century, 344.01, 497.01, 905.01; 18th
century, 256.02, 477.01; articulation, 256.02, 495; fingering, 173.02, 477.03;
ornamentation, 247.01, 256.02, 362, 905.01; T. Stanesby, 477.02; A. Vivaldi,
477.01

Reger, M., 616
Reissiger, C. G., 1075
repeats, 18th century, 469; 19th century, 1031.01; J. S. Bach, 814; L. v. Beethoven, 468, 470; A. d. Cabezón, 868.01; G. Muffat, 744
Reusner, E., 571, 758
rhythm, 207, 723, 725, 900, 1011.01; Baroque, 57, 59, 819, 886, 925, 1018, 1121; 15th century, 201, 389.01, 477; 16th century, 15.01, 201, 202, 236, 358, 477, 636, 1083; 17th century, 25, 96.01, 149.01, 203, 235, 453, 479.02, 605, 808, 922, 949, 1019, 1084; 18th century, 37, 39, 127, 129, 130, 203, 310, 603, 765, 808, 828, 1019, 1084; 19th century, 173.002, 798.01; declamation, 276.01, 1062.01; madrigal, 277, 278; monody, 34.01; notes inégales, 16.01, 54, 55.02, 57, 59, 130, 247, 267, 268, 433, 507, 762, 819, 1019; voice, 824.01; J. S. Bach, 56, 82, 83, 268, 269, 300, 301, 457, 490, 491, 506, 585, 675, 676, 684, 724, 761.01. 764, 775, 799, 827, 882, 883, 924, 1035, 1103.01; L. v. Beethoven, 855, 885, 977.01; J. Blow, 39; J. Brahms, 706; F. Couperin, 679; C. W. Gluck, 702; G. F. Handel, 394, 404, 462, 775, 1106; F. J. Haydn, 855; C. Merulo, 509.01; W. A. Mozart, 855, 884, 885; G. Muffat, 744, 745; H. Purcell, 104, 267; P. Ritter, 295.01; F. Schubert, 287, 318, 705
Richter, F. X., 867
Ritter, P., 295.01
Rosovsky, P. P., 864.01
Rossi, S., 770
Rossini, G., 181.01, 313
Rousseau, J. J., 181

S

Sacchini, A., 213
Salèpico, J., 908
Santa Maria, T. de, 55.02, 434
saxophone, 880
Scarlatti, A., 227, 252
Scarlatti, D., 530, 549
Scheidemann, H., 149.001
Scheidt, S., 645, 915
Schlick, A., 539, 931; tuning, 501.01
Schobert, J., 582
Schubert, F., appoggiatura, 42.01, 817.01, 1078; dynamics, 148; rhythm, 287, 318, 705, 1019.01; tempo, 1019.01; Piano Sonatas, 705, 1020.02; Die Winterreise, 1019.01
Schütz, H., 105, 482, 514, 547, 699, 721, 740.01; Christmas Story, 685; Musicalische Exquien, 686; Passions, 983; Psalms, 283, 875; Symphonia sacrae, 875
Schumann, R., 517, 1001; articulation, 250.001, 348.01; dynamics, 250.001; piano, 117.01, 250.001, 250.01
scordatura, 589; see also individual instruments, tuning
Sechter, S., 1037
Senfl, L., 632, 722
Simpson, C., 773
singing, see voice, comprehensive
Soler, P. A., 527
sonata, keyboard, 635.02; texture, 635.02
spinet, 254.01, see also clavichord, harpsichord, keyboard, piano
Spohr, L., 391
Staden, J., 770
Stamitz, J., 867
Stamitz, K., 866

Stanesby, T., 477.02
Stich, J. V., 709
Stoltzer, T., 403
string instruments, 16th century, 405.03; vibrato, 95.02
Strozzi, G., 497.02
suite, keyboard, 7.01
Sweelinck, J. P., 229.01, 459

T

tactus, 16th century, 173.003, *see also* conducting, rhythm, tempo
Tartini, G., 144, 213, 271.001, 505.01, 1024
Telemann, G. P., 581, 701, 1027
temperament, *see* tuning
tempo, 422.01, 430, 517.01, 520, 640, 641, 697, 754, 900; Renaissance, 623; Baroque, 358.01, 380, 496, 819, 886; 13th century, 411; 14th century, 411; 15th century, 173, 210, 477; 16th century, 173.003, 236, 477, 776, 1009; 17th century, 183, 235, 453, 466, 602, 776, 922, 1084, 1100.01; 18th century, 2, 16, 37, 125, 126, 133, 183, 253.01, 466, 480, 548, 653, 734, 776, 800, 816, 1049, 1084; 19th century, 155, 800, 881, 1031.01; keyboard, 7.01; madrigal, 277; organ, 405.04; rubato, 367.01, 798.01; J. S. Bach, 83, 112, 269, 405.04, 535, 550, 560, 561, 611, 684, 883, 1000; L. v. Beethoven, 85, 87, 221, 251, 352, 576, 717, 780, 977.01, 989, 1062; J. Brahms, 322; D. Buxtehude, 583; M. A. Charpentier, 479.01; F. Chopin, 189, 456, 521, 608, 857, 966.01; A. Corelli, 511; F. Couperin, 679; G. Dufay, 1060; G. F. Handel, 394, 404, 409; J. C. Kerll, 384.01; F. Mendelssohn, 1061; C. Merulo, 509.01; W. A. Mozart, 67, 298, 381, 742, 838, 884, 993, 998, 999; G. Muffat, 743, 744, 745; G. Palestrina, 49; H. Purcell, 42, 104, 832; D. Scarlatti, 530; H. Schütz, 685; R. Schumann, 517, 1001; G. P. Telemann, 701, 1027; T. Tomkins, 180.01; C. M. v. Weber, 518.01
texture, 18th century, 6, 1010; hurdy gurdy, 279.03; keyboard, 635.02, 771, 1010; violin, 809; P. Ritter, 295.01
Théâtres de la Foire, 76.011
theorbo, 17th century, 279.01
thorough bass, *see* basso continuo
timbre, 754; *see also* individual instruments
Tomkins, T., 180.01
trombone choir, 104.01; Moravian music, 104.01
trouvères, rhythm, 1062.01
trumpet, 476.01, 862, 954, 973; Renaissance, 900.01; Baroque, 287.01, 1076.01; articulation, 27, 28; mutes, 29; ornamentation, 31; timbre, 27, 30; tuning, 29; J. S. Bach, 107, 484, 1076.01; H. Berlioz, 1076.01; G. F. Handel, 287.01
Türk, D. G., 1077
tuning, 26, 76, 98, 441, 555, 777.02; 16th century, 683; 17th century, 683; 18th century, 187.02, 911.01; guitar, 447; harpsichord, 312, 436, 794; lute, 246, 271.002, 572, 575; organ, 539; piano, 733; J. S. Bach, 75, 681, 1103; F. Geminiani, 145.01; P. Prelleur, 145.01; A. Schlick, 501.01
tympani, J. S. Bach, 1031.04

V

Vecchi, O., 770, 1066
vega bow, J. S. Bach, 58, 1005, 1029, 1030, 1031
Viadana, L., 1068, 1069
vihuela, 96, 911